BOOK · TWO
PARADE OF PLAYS
FOR YOUR CHURCH

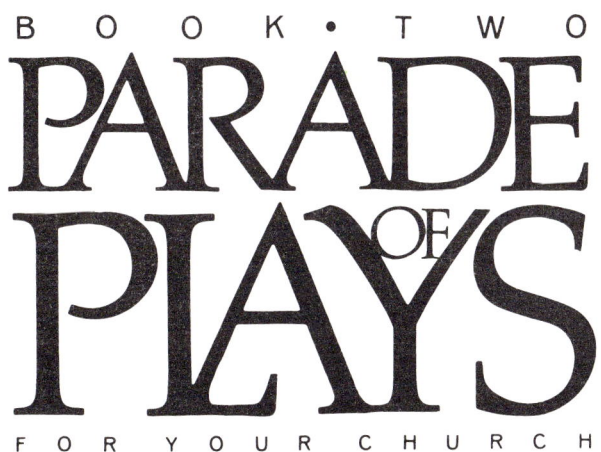

St. Matthew Lutheran Church
125 Main St. PO Box 217
Laurens, N.Y. 13796

David C. Cook Publishing Co.
©1985 Elgin, Illinois—Weston, Ontario

PARADE OF PLAYS 2
For Your Church

© 1985 David C. Cook Publishing Co., Elgin, IL 60120.
Cable address: DCCOOK. Printed in U.S.A. All rights reserved. Plays in this book may be reproduced for use in church without the written permission of the publisher.
Editors: Lucy F. Townsend, Eric Potter, and Kent Lindberg
Cover and text design: Barbara Sheperd Tillman
ISBN: 0-89191-323-8

Preface

When I was in second grade, I acted in my first school play. The night of the performance my mother dressed me in a starched red dress with a white apron she had made just for the occasion. Then she handed me a plate of heart-shaped cookies with red icing. The play was a dramatization of Mother Goose's familiar rhymes. I said eight lines.

I loved it all—my costume, my lines, my cookies, and most of all the excitement of being onstage. I don't remember much about second grade, but I'll never forget that play.

I've seen the same excitement I felt in second grade on the faces of hundreds of costumed kids parading across stage or sanctuary platform. Ah, the power of a play!

Drama is one of the best ways to help people capture the reality of the Christian life. Like Moses, your players can miraculously part the Red Sea. Like Deborah, they can save their people, the chosen of God. And like Peter they can weep over their betrayal of their best friend and Lord. Through such dramatic acts, actors and audience will experience vicariously what it means to "walk by faith and not by sight."

This book is a collection of plays written for you—the Christian leader who may never have tried drama before. **Parade of Plays 1, 2, and 3** contain skits, choral readings, puppet shows, mimes, musicals, and radio dramas which can be used in a variety of church settings. Some are especially for young children. Others can be acted by teens and adults. Also included are helpful suggestions from amateur directors on staging, costumes, cast, etc.

The key to dramatic success is simplicity. Begin with a simple choral reading and then move on to more elaborate productions. Skim through the book looking for plays that sound interesting. Then stop and dig more deeply. Don't forget to read carefully the staging and costuming suggestions. May God bless you with much joy as you act out His story!

Lucy Townsend, Ph.D.

Table of Contents

The Bells of Christmas — 6
by Marjie Mehlis
(Christmas program for children and teens)

Children's Home — 13
by Eric Potter
(Christmas play for children and teens)

Light of the World — 21
by Karen Burton Mains
(Christmas choral reading for teens and adults)

History in Hand — 26
by Annie and Steve Wamberg
(Four puppet plays for children and young teens)

Fabulous Forum on Prayer — 49
by Jim Townsend

Fabulous Forum on Faith and Works — 53
by Kent Lindberg
(Two dramatic panel discussions for teens)

In the Beginning — 58
by David and Becca Toht
(Scripture-based choral reading for children)

If We Had Been There — 71
by Marilee Zdenek, adapted by Ramona Warren
(Easter choral reading for teens)

On Death Row — 74
by Karen Burton Mains
(Missionary drama for teens and adults)

Paul — 86
by Jeanne Murray Walker
(Dramatic Biblical play for teens)

THE BELLS OF CHRISTMAS
A Christmas Tableau
by Marjie Mehlis

"The Bells of Christmas," written for the entire Sunday school, is a traditional Christmas play challenging the Church to focus on Christ during the Christmas season. It includes the major events of the Christmas story in tableau while narrators read or explain the significance of each scene.

A tableau is a useful art form because it can be adapted to many age levels.
- Children who cannot read or do not want to act can wear costumes and pose each scene, holding it throughout the narration.
- Choir songs can be assigned to various age-level classes. For example, preschoolers might sing "Away in a Manger." Primaries might sing "O Little Town of Bethlehem."
- Parts may be read rather than memorized.
- The number of parts can be adjusted to the size of your cast. If you have many children, you might divide narrator's and reader's parts among a number of children. If your cast is small, assign both narrator's and reader's parts to one person.

CAST:
Narrator
Reader
Sally Smith
Don Brown
Johnny Smith
Voice of God
Angel
Mary
Joseph
Three Wise Men
Shepherds
Santa Claus with bell
Scribe
Herod

Tableau Directions:
Players should position themselves onstage and remain frozen. You might beam a spotlight on them. Then the light should be switched off and the scene changed.

Music Needed:
Organ (or piano)
Female Solo: "O Holy Night"
Male Trio: "We Three Kings"

Sound Effects Needed:
Sleigh Bells
Cash Register
Church Bell
Thunder or Gong

Suggested Choir Numbers:
"I Heard the Bells on Christmas Day"
"O Little Town of Bethlehem"
"While Shepherds Watched Their Flocks by Night"
"Joy to the World"
"Away in a Manger"

CHOIR (or the organ): "I Heard the Bells on Christmas Day" (first verse).

(Santa comes across stage ringing bell. He freezes center stage back.)

SOUND: (Sleigh bells drown out end of hymn.)

NARRATOR: It's now the Christmas season. Girls squeal as their toboggans whiz downhill. Children dance with excitement—waiting to see what they will get for Christmas. The Browns happily decorate their tree. Across town, Sue Jones puts a fruit cake into the oven. The city is hectic with last minute Christmas preparations. The Salvation Army Santa Claus rings his bell. (sound of Santa's bell) Sally Smith and Don Brown trudge from store to store. They enter Carsen's. Cash register jangles up a sale.

SOUND: (cash register)

SALLY: Christmas cards are reduced.

SOUND: (thunder or gong)

VOICE: It is my wish that My day should be a holy day. Have you left Me, the Christ, out of Christmas?

(Santa leaves stage.)

NARRATOR: Oh, what has happened to Christmas? Are sleigh bells and Santa Claus and cash registers really Christmas? Two thousand years ago an angel visited a young Jewish girl named Mary in a city of Galilee. For her, Christmas was a holy day.

(Mary, Jesus' mother, kneels on stage left.)

SOLO: (Female vocalist sings [or organ, flute, or other instrument plays] first verse of "O Holy Night.")

READER: Now in the sixth month the angel Gabriel was sent from God unto a city of Galilee, named Nazareth, to a virgin betrothed to a man whose name was Joseph, of the house of David; and the virgin's name was Mary. And he said unto her,

ANGEL: Fear not, Mary: for thou hast found favor with God. And behold, thou shalt conceive in thy womb, and bring forth a son, and shalt call his name Jesus. He shall be great, and shall be called the Son of the Most High: and the Lord God shall give unto him the throne of his father David: and he shall reign over the house of Jacob for ever; and of his kingdom there shall be no end.

MARY: How shall this be, seeing I know not a man?

ANGEL: The Holy Spirit shall come upon thee, and the power of the Most High shall overshadow thee: 'wherefore also the holy thing which is begotten shall be called the Son of God.

MARY: Behold, the handmaid of the Lord; be it unto me according to thy word. . . . My soul doth magnify the Lord, and my spirit hath rejoiced in God my Saviour. For he hath looked upon the low estate of his handmaid: For behold, from henceforth all generations shall call me blessed.

(Organ plays end line of "O Holy Night." Mary leaves stage.)

(Girl and small boy come onstage. They pretend to be talking. They freeze stage right.)

NARRATOR: But do we call Mary blessed? Tonight as Johnny settles into bed, we hear him plead with Sally, his sister.

JOHNNY: Please tell me the Christmas story. Please.

SALLY: O.K., Johnny.

JOHNNY: Then I'll go to sleep.

SALLY: " 'Twas the night before Christmas and all through the house, not a creature was stirring, not even a mouse. The stockings were hung by the chimney with care, in hopes that St. Nicholas soon would be there. And Mommy in her kerchief and I in my cap were just settling our brains for a long winter's nap. When out on the lawn there arose such a clatter . . . ."

SOUND: *(thunder or gong)*

VOICE: It is My wish that the Christmas story should tell of My birth. Do not make it only a tale of Santa Claus.

(Boy and girl leave stage. Mary and Joseph sit at the manger on left side of stage.)

NARRATOR: What about Christ's birth? Is that why we celebrate Christmas? Perhaps we should go back nearly two thousand years to the town of Bethlehem.

CHOIR *(or organ)*: *(sing first verse of "O Little Town of Bethlehem")*

READER: Now it came to pass in those days, there went out a decree from Caesar Augustus, that all the world should be enrolled. This was the first enrollment made when Quirinius was governor of Syria. And all went to enroll themselves, every one to his own city. And Joseph also went up from Galilee, out of the city of Nazareth, into Judea, to the city of David, which is called Bethlehem, because he was of the house and family of David; to enroll himself with Mary, who was betrothed to him, being great with child. And it came to pass, while they were there, the days were fulfilled that she should be delivered. And she brought forth her firstborn son; and she wrapped him in swaddling clothes, and laid him in a manger, because there was no room for them in the inn.

CHOIR: *(sing "Away in a Manger")*

NARRATOR: There was no room for Jesus in Bethlehem. Do we leave room for Him now? What place does Christ have in your Christmas celebration?

(Shepherds look up and point on right side of stage.)

CHOIR: *("While Shepherds Watched Their Flocks by Night")*

READER: There were shepherds in the same country abiding in the field, and keeping watch by night over their flock. And an angel of the Lord stood by them, and the glory of the Lord shone round about them: and they were sore afraid. And the angel said unto them,

ANGEL: Be not afraid; for behold, I bring you good tidings of great joy which shall be to all the people: for there is born to you this day in the city of David a Saviour, who is Christ the Lord. And this is the sign unto you: Ye shall find a babe wrapped in swaddling clothes, and lying in a manger.

READER: And then suddenly there was with the angel a multitude of the heavenly host saying,

ANGEL: Glory to God in the highest, and on earth peace among men.

READER: And it came to pass, when the angels went away from them into heaven, the shepherds said one to another,

SHEPHERD: Let us now go even unto Bethlehem, and see this thing that is come to pass, which the Lord hath made known unto us.

(Shepherds join Mary, Joseph, and manger.)

READER: And they came with haste, and found both Mary and Joseph, and the babe lying in the manger. And when they saw it, they made known concerning the saying which was spoken to them about this child. And all that heard it wondered at the things which were spoken unto them by the shepherds. But Mary kept all these sayings, pondering them in her heart. And the shepherds returned, glorifying and praising God for all the things that they had heard and seen.

ORGAN: *(quietly play "While Shepherds Watched Their Flocks" as transition)*

NARRATOR: After that, the shepherds immediately

went out and told others of the birth of Christ. Do we tell anyone now? Or perhaps I should say, What do we tell people now?

(modern girl with young boy again, include a package wrapped with a big bow)

JOHNNY: Hey, Sally, guess what? I've got a neat secret.
SALLY: What is it? Have you been into something?
JOHNNY: No! I didn't do anything bad. I just saw a big package in Mama's room.
SALLY: And?
JOHNNY: I think it's for me.
SALLY: Is that the big secret?
JOHNNY: Well, sort of.
SALLY: Maybe it's for me!
JOHNNY: I hope not. I want whatever it is!
SOUND: *(thunder or gong)*
VOICE: It is My wish that you should give to others. Remember that it is more blessed to give than to receive. *(Boy and girl leave stage.)*
(Wise Men and Herod on throne [chair], middle stage rear)

MALE TRIO *(or a musical instrument)*: *(sing "We Three Kings")*
READER: Now when Jesus was born in Bethlehem of Judea in the days of Herod the king, behold, Wise Men from the east came to Jerusalem, saying,
MAN: Where is he that is born King of the Jews? For we saw his star in the east, and came to worship him.
READER: And when Herod the king heard it, he was troubled, and all Jerusalem with him. And gathering together all the chief priests and scribes of the people, he inquired of them where the Christ should be born. And they said unto him.
SCRIBE: In Bethlehem of Judea: for thus it is written through the prophet, and thou Bethlehem, land of Judah, Art in no wise least among the princes of Judah: for out of thee shall come forth a governor, who shall be shepherd of my people Israel.
READER: Then Herod privily called the Wise Men, and learned of them exactly

what time the star appeared. And he sent them to Bethlehem, and said,

HEROD: Go and search out exactly concerning the young child; and when ye have found him, bring me word, that I also may come and worship him.

READER: And they, having heard the king, went their way; and lo, the star, which they saw in the east, went before them, till it came and stood over where the young child was. And when they saw the star, they rejoiced with exceeding great joy. And they came into the house and saw the young child with Mary his mother; and they fell down and worshipped him; and opening their treasures they offered unto him gifts, gold and frankincense and myrrh. And being warned of God in a dream that they should not return to Herod, they departed into their own country another way.

ORGAN: *("We Three Kings")*
NARRATOR: Yes, the Wise Men went to see Christ and received guidance from God. It's Christmas. Where do we go?
DON: Tobogganing.
SALLY: Shopping.
DON: Visiting.
SALLY: Caroling.
CHOIR: *("I Heard the Bells on Christmas Day")*

(Modern girl and small boy kneel before manger. Mary and Joseph stand to one side.)

SOUND: *(Sleigh bells, cash register, Santa's bell, church bells all ringing in montage effect. Finally the church bells win out.)*
NARRATOR: The church's bell calls us to worship. It's Christmas eve. The Christ Child has been born for us.
VOICE: I was despised and rejected of men.
NARRATOR: Let us worship Him.
CHOIR: *(sing "Joy to the World"—two verses joyously as close)*

CHILDREN'S HOME
An Allegorical Christmas Play
By Eric Potter

This allegorical play can be performed by kids from first through eighth grade. Its subject matter is serious enough to be meaningful to senior highs and adults.

Staging:
The play can be performed on a regular stage or in a church auditorium. Chorus should stand (and sit) in choir loft if it's in front of the church, otherwise to the right or the left of the stage. Stage left should lead to "other" parts of the orphanage and stage right lead "outside."

Costuming:
Orphans should wear old ragged clothes, mess up their hair, and smudge their faces—they'll love it. Policemen should wear blue if possible and maybe a badge made from cardboard and foil. The chorus may want to dress as orphans or in matching outfits (i.e., navy blue skirts and trousers, and white shirts).

Props:
You can use many or few, depending on your resources. A number of low tables could be used both for the dining room scene, and as beds for the night scene. Governor Good needs a wrapped Christmas present and a cane. You will also need an orphanage sign. A whip for Mister Fiend would add a nice touch.

Cast:
You should use older kids for Mister Fiend, Governor Good, Maria, and Joe. Bethel should be young. The chorus can be as big or small as you want. If you are low on actors you can cut the henchmen and policemen by one and have orphans double up on bit parts.

Mister Fiend—director of the orphanage
Governor Good—the hero
Maria—older orphan girl
Joe—older orphan boy—friends with Maria
Bethel—young orphan girl
Judy—older orphan girl—mean
Mister Fiend's Henchmen I, II, III *(use 2 girls, 1 boy)*
Policemen *(use 2 girls)*
Orphans *(Around 10 including Joe, Maria, Judy, and Bethel. Some have small speaking parts.)*
Chorus—must be able to sing and recite together
Stage hands—some kids may prefer making scene adjustments and doing lighting and sound.

SCENE 1

Setting: dining room with side entrance (stage right), low tables. A sign by the side door says: "Wanderers Orphanage, Mister Fiend, Director."
(Before lights come on, Chorus *begins singing "I'm Just a Poor, Wayfaring Stranger" (available in* Hymns for the Living Church, *1974). Sing first verse using the line: "I'm going there to see my mother." During second verse lights come on, children are sweeping and scrubbing floor, some are setting tables, others cooking, some carrying in wood, and others shoveling the sidewalk. In the second verse, chorus should sing the line: "I'm going there to see my father." Chorus stops singing. Orphans continue working for a few moments in silence.)*

CHORUS: The sun rises and sets and rises and sets. We eat and work and sleep and eat and work and sleep. We are tired and we want to stop, tired, we want to stop, want to stop. Because everything seems empty.
(Older boys begin chanting.): empty, empty, empty, empty . . .
(Girls and younger boys say the following part.): Mean Mister Fiend treats us like slaves. *(Shout the next part and pause between each phrase.)* Sweep the floor. Scrub the clothes. Chop wood. Shovel snow.
(in unison): We want to stop.
(Enter, from stage left, Joe and another boy carrying a small Christmas tree. Children stop working and gather around tree. Boys set it up in the corner.)

JOE *(excited)*: It's Christmas Eve! Let's decorate the tree.
(Kids cheer and begin decorating tree, all except Judy who sneaks

off unnoticed. Enter Mr. Fiend and his Henchmen led by Judy.)

JUDY: Over there. *(points to kids around tree)*

FIEND: What's the meaning of this? Why aren't you working? And what is that thing? *(points to tree)*

JOE: It's a Christmas tree, sir. Today's Christmas Eve, and . . .

FIEND: Quiet! Don't ever use that word here. *(to henchmen 2 and 3)* Get rid of that branch. *(to henchman 1)* Bring him with me. *(points at Joe)* The rest of you get back to work. *(kicks at a kid) (Fiend and henchman exit stage left dragging Joe by arm. Children resume work)*

CHORUS *(boys resume work chant, others)*: Poor, poor Joe, where did he go? The Fiend will box his ears.

SCENE TWO

Setting: dining room, kids are milling around. Joe's head is bandaged.
(A bell rings. Kids hurry to their seats. Henchman 1 enters from stage left and addresses the orphans.)

HENCHMAN 1: Silence! *(with sneering sarcasm)* What would you little dears like for supper?
(the following items called out by various orphans)
Chocolate chip cookies! Pizza! Ice cream! Tacos! Apple pie!

HENCHMAN 1: Well, you can't have them. You get liver. *(groans from orphans)* Now get in line. *(Makes first kid in line serve food. Judy should be close to the end of the line. Chorus speaks as kids go through the line.)*

CHORUS: We hate liver. We hate liver. We have it for breakfast. We have it for lunch. We have it for supper. Every day, every week, every year. Liver—yech!

(Henchman stops line when it's Judy's turn.)

HENCHMAN 1: Are you the one that told on the other children?

JUDY *(frightened)*: Yes.

HENCHMAN 1: Then you don't have to eat this slop. Your reward is to dine with Mr. Fiend himself. He'll give you all the spaghetti and soda pop and chocolate cake that you can eat.

(Exit stage left henchman and Judy, rest of children finish through line. Lights go down.)

SCENE THREE

Setting: dormitory room (tables become kids' beds). Lights should be dim.
(All the children are lying down except Maria and Joe who talk quietly.)

MARIA: Does your head hurt a lot, Joe?
JOE: Some, but it's not too bad.
MARIA: I wish we could get away.
JOE: Me, too. But we can't. Believe me, I tried before.
MARIA: What happened?
JOE: Nothing. I ended up back here. They found me and brought me back.
MARIE: Where'd you go?
JOE: I ran through the woods till I came to the edge of a cliff. There was a stream running through the canyon. I could see fields on the other side, green fields with white dots. I thought I saw people walking around between the dots, so I shouted hello but no one ever answered.

(Maria lets out a huge yawn.)

JOE: I guess we better go to sleep.
MARIE: Yeah, maybe we'll be lucky and have good dreams.
JOE: What do you dream about?
MARIE: I'm not sure. A face sometimes.
JOE: What kind of face?
MARIE: I think it's a mother's face. I don't know what a mother looks like, but I think it's my mother.

(silence)

Oh, well, good night, Joe.
JOE: Good night, Maria.

(They lie down.)

CHORUS: The orphans slip into a troubled sleep. They cry and shout at bad dreams. Their restless night noises rise like smoke from a fire.

(Sing first verse of "O Come, O Come Emmanuel."

A young child begins crying. Maria wakes up and goes and kneels beside Bethel's bed.)

MARIA: What's wrong, Bethel?
BETHEL: I had a dream.
MARIA: A bad dream?
BETHEL *(shakes her head no)*: A good dream, about a man with a happy face and a big house with dogs and cats and a big Christmas tree, bigger than the man.
MARIA: But why are you crying if it was a happy dream?
BETHEL: Because I woke up here.

(Maria puts her back to sleep. Enter Henchman 2 with flashlight. Walks around shining light like a prison guard.)

SCENE FOUR

Setting: empty cafeteria, bright sunlight.

CHORUS: It's Christmas morning, but it's just another day at Wanderers Orphanage. Or is it?

(Enter from stage left, Mr. Fiend and his henchmen. They stop at center stage and talk together silently. Someone knocks on the door. Fiend and friends keep talking. The person knocks louder. The center group stops. Someone knocks again.)

FIEND: Well, get the door.

(Henchman 3 answers the door. Good steps in boldly, carrying a large present under one arm.)

GOOD *(in booming voice)*: Good morning and Merry Christmas! I'm Governor Good. *(holds out his hand but Fiend won't shake it)*
FIEND *(suspiciously)*: What's that? *(nods toward present)*
GOOD: It's a Christmas *(Fiend covers his ears at the word.)* present for the orphans.
FIEND: Fine, fine, we'll take care of it. *(Takes package from Good who hesitates to give it up. Fiend hands it to Henchman 2 and addresses him privately with his back to Good, so Good "can't" hear him.)* Here, put this little prize somewhere safe where those grubby brats can't get to it.

(Exit Henchman 2, stage left. Fiend continues talking silently

to his other henchmen. Then he notices that Good is still there.)

FIEND (rudely): What are you still hanging around for?

GOOD: Mind if I look around a bit? I grew up here, you know. I'm surprised you don't remember me.

FIEND (looks hard at Good): Well, I don't. (looks straight at audience and confides) Orphans all look the same anyway. (turns back to Good and shrugs his shoulders) Suit yourself. Good day.

(Exit Good stage right. Fiend and henchmen exit stage left.)

(Enter all orphans with work tools. Bethel and Maria on stage left. Maria is sweeping, and Bethel is holding dustpan.)

CHORUS (All chant.): Empty, empty, empty, empty . . .

(Enter Good from stage right. He stops and looks around. Children stop work and stare. Chorus stops chant. Only Maria keeps sweeping. Bethel is dangling dustpan at side and pointing at Good.)

MARIA: Come on, Bethel, pay attention. (sweeps a little) Bethel! (Maria looks up at Bethel and then to where she's pointing.)

BETHEL: It's him.

MARIA: Who?

BETHEL: The happy face man in my dream.

GOOD: Merry Christmas, children! (They stare blankly.) But look at you! You're working on Christmas. (Good looks around in unbelief. Joe steps forward, curious but also protective.)

JOE (pause): Who are you? And what do you want?

GOOD: I'm called Governor Good. (with determination) Someone's got to do something about all this.

MARIA: But who, and what can they do?

GOOD: I'll tell you who—me. And as for what—why, I'll adopt you.

ORPHAN 1: What's adopt?

GOOD: It means that I'm taking you to live with me in my house.

ORPHAN 2: Is it as big as here?

GOOD: Bigger. It's a mansion with lots of rooms.

BETHEL: And do you have dogs and cats?

GOOD *(to Bethel)*: Lots of them.

(Orphans all start to cheer and clap. Enter Fiend and Henchmen from stage left. Children see them and stop cheering.)

FIEND: What in Heaven's name is going on in here?

GOOD: I'm adopting these children.

FIEND: Impossible . . . You can't . . . Impossible.

GOOD: But I'm going to.

FIEND *(stands directly in front of Good)*: You can't, I said. They're mine! Mine! I own them!

GOOD: You don't own anybody. I'm taking them home and you can't stop me.

(Fiend stomps on Good's foot. Good yells in pain and hops up and down on his other foot.)

FIEND: Now get out of here before I get your other foot. *(Good grabs his cane and hits Fiend on the head. Fiend falls to floor. Good threatens henchmen with cane. They crouch around Fiend.)*

GOOD: Someone call the police.

(Exit stage left one orphan. Sound of sirens. Police enter stage right.)

POLICEMAN 1 *(doesn't see Good)*: Okay, what seems to be the problem here? *(sees Fiend)* Hey, what in the world . . . *(looks at kids suspiciously)* Who's responsible for this? *(points at Fiend)*

GOOD *(steps up from background)*: I am.

POLICEMAN 1: Oh, Governor Good. Sorry, I didn't see you. What should I do?

GOOD *(pointing at Fiend and helpers)*: Take Mr. Fiend and his henchmen and throw them in jail. Then throw away the key.

(Exit stage right policemen dragging Fiend and crowd. Fiend clutching head.)

GOOD *(dusting off his hands)*: Well, that's settled.
(Good turns to leave.)

MARIA: Wait, aren't we coming with you?

GOOD: Not right now. I have to get things ready. But don't worry, I'm sending my limousine to pick you up. It will be here before dark.

CHORUS: *(sings first verse of "Joy to the World")*

SCENE FIVE

Setting: late afternoon, stage dim but not dark. Orphans (except Bethel) sitting around bored and sad.

(Chorus sings "I'm Just a Poor, Wayfaring Stranger." This time use the line: "I'm going there to see my Savior.")

ORPHAN 1: I'm hungry.
ORPHAN 2: Me, too.
ORPHAN 3: I don't think he's coming back.
MARIA: Of course he is. *(pause, then doubtfully)* He promised.
JOE: He's got to.

(Enter Bethel from stage left, dragging Good's cane.)

MARIA: Hey, what is that, Bethel?
BETHEL: It's his.
JOE: Whose?
BETHEL: The man's.
MARIA: The governor's cane! He left it.
JOE: Then he is coming. If he left his cane he has to come.

(Sound of a horn honking.)

ORPHAN 4 *(stage right on tiptoes as if looking out a window)*: He's here.

(Chorus sings first verse of "O Come, All Ye Faithful." Orphans should sing with the chorus and exit stage right one by one. As song ends, slowly dim the lights.)

THE END

LIGHT OF THE WORLD
A Christmas Choral Reading
by Karen Burton Mains

The Light of the World is what Christmas is all about. God sent His Son to light up our world so we wouldn't have to live in darkness anymore. This is the message God wants the whole world to know; and this is the message you should try to get across as you read this script to the congregation. For the greatest impact, it should be presented at night.

In order for your reading to go smoothly, don't read the reader's instructions which are italicized and in parentheses. Don't read the Scripture references aloud either.

All Bible verses quoted in this script have been taken from the Revised Standard Version of the Bible.

As you practice, experiment with different kinds of light. To make this choral reading more meaningful, you might use lanterns, flashlights, spotlights, strobe lights, or candles.

Cast:
Chorus
Readers *(five)*
Male Voice *(use chorus member)*
Female Voice *(use chorus member)*

MALE VOICE: For centuries men have argued over light.
READER 1: Pythagoras: *(short pause)* Every visible object emits a steady stream of particles.
READER 2: Aristotle: *(short pause)* Light travels in waves.
READER 3: Isaac Newton: *(short pause)* Light is like a shower of particles shot from a luminous object, with each particle traveling in a straight line until it is refracted, absorbed, reflected, or somehow acted upon.
READER 4: Thomas Young: *(short pause)* Light travels in waves. This hypothesis can be proven by beaming light from one point, at a board through which two small holes have been drilled . . .
FEMALE VOICE *(interrupts in an awed, hushed voice)*: What is light? What is this mysterious glowing element that gushes forth in so many colors and varieties from the sun, from bulbs, from candles, fireflies, and fireworks? What is this shimmer . . . filtering through the morning trees? What is this twilight of late afternoon?
MALE VOICE: For centuries men have argued over light.
FEMALE VOICE: But what is it? What is this burst of color captured in a crystal goblet? What is this searing glare of searchlight?
READER 4: The Artist: *(short pause)* Hue and value, canvas or paper, oil or watercolor—none of these matter. Painting is all a matter of light.
READER 5: Webster's Dictionary: *(short pause)* Light—the energy which is transmitted at a velocity of about 186,000 miles per second by wavelike or vibrational motion.
FEMALE VOICE: But what is light?
CHORUS: What is light? What is light? What is light? What is light? What is light? What is light?
MALE VOICE: In 1905, Albert Einstein argued that the wave theory of light

might be incomplete; that light might have some of the characteristics of a particle after all. Experiments indicated that light, this commonplace but mysterious stuff which fills the universe, is wavelike and particlelike at the same time—with two different characteristics of the same thing.

CHORUS: Now the light has come! The light has come into the world! Today we celebrate its coming!

READER 1: The people who sat in darkness have seen a great light . . .

READER 2: And for those who sat in the region and shadow of death light has dawned (Matthew 4:16).

MALE VOICE: But for centuries man has argued over light . . .

Turn off the lights. Continue in darkness.

CHORUS (*arguing, shouting—you should divide the chorus*):
MAN!
GOD!
MAN!
GOD!
Man/God! God/Man!
Man only! God all!

FEMALE VOICE: What is light? What is light?

MALE VOICE: This light also has two different characteristics. This light is both God and man. This light is the Son who was given *(slight pause).* But ask not what it is; ask what it does.

READER 3: What does light do?

FEMALE VOICE: It shines. It glows. It gleams.

CHORUS: It lights up the darkness!

Turn on lights.

READER 4: And God said, "Let there be light"; and there was light. And God saw that the light was good (Genesis 1:3, 4a).

READER 5: And if one look[s] to the land, behold, darkness and distress; and the light is darkened by its clouds (Isaiah 5:30).

MALE VOICE: Zechariah the priest: *(short pause)* The day shall dawn upon us from on high to give light to those who sit in darkness and in the shadow of death (Luke 1:78, 79a).

MALE VOICE *(short pause)*: Mine eyes have seen thy salvation which thou hast prepared in the presence of all peoples, a light for revelation to the Gentiles, and for glory to Israel (Luke 2:30-32).

READERS: The true light that enlightens every man was coming into the world (John 1:9).

CHORUS: Light-light, light-light, light-light . . .

MALE VOICE: I am the light of the world; he who follows me will not walk in darkness, but will have the light of life (John 8:12).

FEMALE VOICE *(whispering)*: Jesus is the light. Jesus is the light.

CHORUS: Jesus is the light,
The light of the world.
Jesus is the light,
The light of the world.
Jesus is the light,
The light of the world.
He's ever shining in my soul.

READER 1: Come, let us walk in the light of the Lord (Isaiah 2:5).

READER 2: That you may declare the wonderful deeds of him who called you out of darkness into his marvelous light (I Peter 2:9).

READER 3: Awake now, O sleeper, and arise from the dead, and Christ shall give you light.

MALE VOICE: For centuries men have argued over light . . .

CHORUS: The light has come
Into the world.
(Turn off the lights.)
But men loved darkness
Rather than light.
Because their deeds were evil.

MALE VOICE: Yes, men have argued over this light that came into the world. They have argued for centuries. They have tried to hide the light. They have hunted the followers of that light, imprisoning them in the deepest of dungeons. They have even scoffed at the light, pretending it wasn't there. But they should have known from that time long ago, when they nailed the light to a tree, and when it flickered

for a moment in eternity—
(short pause)
(Turn on lights.)

that the light from God cannot be put out.

CHORUS *(whispering)*: I have come as light into the world *(louder)*, that whoever believes in me may not remain in darkness (John 12:46).

READER 4 *(shouting)*: The people who walked in darkness have seen a great light!

CHORUS *(whispering)*: I have come to give sight to the blind.

READER 5 *(shouting)*: The true light that enlightens every man has come into the world!

FEMALE VOICE: Jesus is the light! The light of the world!

CHORUS: Jesus is the light,
The light of the world.
Jesus is the light,
The light of the world.
Jesus is the light,
The light of the world.
He's shining in my soul.

(Sing "O Little Town of Bethlehem.")

HISTORY IN HAND
A Church History Puppet Play
by Annie and Steve Wamberg

Most of us are incredibly ignorant about church history and that's too bad because there's a lot to be learned from our predecessors in the Christian faith. The following four puppet plays depict important church leaders ministering in their generations.

"Order in the Church! Order in the Church!" sheds light on the early church after the close of the Book of Acts.

"An Old St. Bernard Teaches New Tricks" shows how one Christian turned evil into good during the Middle Ages.

"Back to the Basics" reveals Martin Luther's contribution to the Reformation (1500-1650).

"The Gospel Going and Coming" depicts a major figure in the Great Awakening, a time of revival between 1650 and 1850.

Each puppet skit lasts from 10-15 minutes and can be performed in a classroom, children's opening worship, or sanctuary. Through these plays, puppeteers and audiences will learn much about church history.

Puppets You'll Need:
Irv Inchworm
The Kid
The Apostle John
Polycarp
Augustine
Bowser—The Kid's Pet St. Bernard
Bernard
Bruno
Martin Luther
Huldreich Zwingli
Teresa of Avila
John Wesley
Spangenberg
Jonathan Edwards

Suggestion for St. Bernard dog puppet: Use a large sock. Put fishing weights inside the side of his lower jaw and sew in place. What's a St. Bernard dog without jowls!?!

A SIMPLE, CHEAP PUPPET STAGE

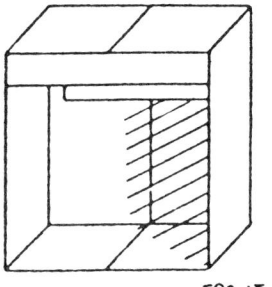

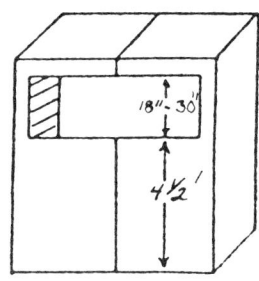

You'll need two refrigerator boxes for this stage. You will be making the right side of the stage from one box and the left side from the other box. Cut the inside side from each box, and most of the back. Leave about six inches at the top on the back for stability. Don't leave any cardboard on the side or bottom of the back because it would get in the way of your puppeteers. Be sure to leave the bottoms in the boxes or your stage will lose its shape.

The basic measurements are given in the drawings. The stage opening should be about four and one-half feet high. You might want to adjust that height if your teens are exceptionally short or tall.

Make your opening as wide as you can. Three inches on each side will give enough support.

Duct tape works well to fasten the boxes together. You may also want to reinforce the stage with furring strips along the edges of the opening, at the bottom along the front, and at the top across the back.

Lighting for puppetry is important. You'll want to check out the lighting available in the room in which you will be performing. Lighting from the front is best, but lighting from overhead will work if the top is removed from the stage.

Stage Scenery: If you're planning to perform these sketches for an audience, you'll want to make some scenery for your puppet stage. Have some of your teens who are interested start on it now. They'll need to work on it outside of practice time, so be sure they're willing to commit the time.

Look over all the scripts, and decide what scenery you want made. You may be able to use the same scenery for several different scenes.

One good type of scenery is painted paper or cloth rolled on a wooden dowel. A spring-loaded window shade also works well. Either one can be temporarily attached at the top of the stage and the scenery rolled down.

A more 3-D effect can be achieved by painting cardboard or Masonite and attaching it to the stage. It can also be made to stand by itself on a base.

ORDER IN THE CHURCH! ORDER IN THE CHURCH!

Cast:
Irv Inchworm
The Kid
John
Polycarp
Augustine

(Light is up only on left side of stage. The Kid enters, dressed up as if having just come from Sunday school.)

KID *(calling offstage)*: Thanks for the ride! See you at youth group! *(turns toward audience, but talking to self)* Sunday school sure was interesting today . . . I like hearing about the early church, and the apostles like Paul setting up churches . . . Wonder what it would have been like if Paul had started our church here? . . . Hey, I wonder who did start our church here? . . . Who kept the church going after New Testament times? Somebody had to, right? . . . I guess I won't find out today, anyway . . . . Wonder what's for dinner?

IRV *(voice only)*: Psst . . . Kid . . . Hey, Kid!

KID *(turning from side to side)*: What's that? Who? . . . where? . . . what?

(Lights up center stage as Irv enters there.)

IRV: It's me. The name's Irv.

KID: Oh, wait 'til I tell Mom about this! The exterminator's warranty has another month on it . . .

IRV: Slow down, Kid! I'm not your normal creepy-crawly type of creature. *(Irv moves toward Kid until at left center then stops.)*

KID: Oh, yeah? Prove it!

IRV: You're talking to me, right?

KID *(embarrassed pause and chuckle)*: Uh . . . guess so.

IRV: I'm an inchworm. A special inchworm. You may be aware that we inchworms are famous for measuring.

KID: I wasn't aware. . . .

IRV: You will be soon. As I was saying, we inchworms are famous for measuring. We used to settle for simple measurements of length, but when they started making digital rulers, we had to change.

KID: Digital rulers?
IRV: Brutal, isn't it? So now we measure other things. Intelligence, for one thing. That's how I knew it would be worth my time to talk to you. Time . . . that's another thing we measure.
KID: Don't let this get you down, but they have digital watches now, too.
IRV: No, no. Not that kind of time measurement. We measure historical time lines. We're able to tell you all about past events.
KID: Really?
IRV: No kidding, Kid. And I heard you talking about who kept the church going after New Testament times. Thought I could help you out.
KID: You? How?
IRV: Imagination . . . information . . . and connections with the scriptwriter.
KID: Huh?
IRV: Never mind, Kid. Just enjoy it, OK?

(Lights flash off and on several times, then stay on. Scenery could reflect a small island setting.)

KID: An island, huh?
IRV: Yeah. Welcome to Patmos.
KID: So what happens here?
IRV: Unfortunately, not vacations or resort living. We're here to meet someone who's really been through some hard things. He traveled setting up churches for almost 60 years. When he started out his brother worked with him, but was executed for his Christian faith shortly after they began their missionary work. This man worked closely with a number of friends who knew Jesus also, but now he's the only one of that band still living. Most of the others have suffered and died because of their belief in Christ. He's been persecuted continuously for spreading the Gospel. In fact, he's on this island because the Roman government has forced him into exile here for the rest of his life.
KID: Wow! I'd say he's been through it! Who is he?
IRV: The apostle John. Here he comes now.

(John enters from offstage left.)
JOHN: I know everyone on Patmos . . . or at least I thought I did. But I don't think we've met. I'm John.
IRV: We're just visiting, sir. That's why we haven't met.
KID: I didn't know you'd been through so much persecution . . . losing your friends and brother, suffering because of Jesus, and now you're exiled on this rocky island . . .
JOHN: Oh, young friend, many others have been through much more. The Church has spread because it had to. Christians were thrown out of cities, and forced to move elsewhere. The Roman government didn't understand us. Some emperors demanded to be worshiped, and we couldn't do that—Jesus alone is our Lord. When we refused to worship the emperor, he stiffened the persecution against us. Some emperors even tracked Christians down to kill them. Nero resented us so greatly that he accused Christians of setting Rome on fire. As a result, many Christians were crucified or lashed to a pole and burned. We think Peter was crucified upside down about then, and Paul beheaded. And now I am the last of the original twelve still living. But the Gospel of the Lord Jesus shall outlive me, you can be sure of that!
KID: I never knew this stuff . . . I just never knew.
IRV: There's more, Kid. Thank you for your time today, sir. We must be on our way now.
JOHN: Quite all right. Always glad to see some new faces.
(Lights flash off and on, resting at fully up. Scenery could reflect ancient small city.)
IRV: Keep a low profile, Kid. They're after the man we're about to visit.
KID: Why? What'd he do?
IRV: He's a church leader.
KID: That's his only crime?
IRV: Remember what John said, Kid? It still holds true here in the middle of the second century.
(Polycarp enters from right.)

POLYCARP: Strangers, I see. But no need to be. My name is Polycarp. Tell me, has Rome sent you?
IRV: No, we're strangers to the Empire.
POLYCARP: Are you strangers to Christ Jesus?
KID: No. I'm a Christian!
POLYCARP: Such boldness for one so young!
KID: Boldness?
POLYCARP: That confession has cost so many so much . . . and the persecution still continues. I expect to be taken to Rome any day now to be tried and killed. I'm Bishop here, and they'll want to make an example of me.
KID: Why don't you hide?
POLYCARP: Because I am not ashamed of the Gospel of Christ. I have served Him for over 80 years and He has never done me wrong. I trust Him to go with me through whatever I must face—it would be a privilege to suffer for my Lord.
KID *(very seriously)*: That's real dedication.
POLYCARP: I'm on my way to the house where our church meets. Would you like to join me?
IRV: No, thank you. I'm afraid we must be moving on.
POLYCARP: So be it. God go with you.
KID: And with you!

(Polycarp exits left as lights flash off and on. When lights rest at fully up, scenery could show another ancient city.)

KID: Irv, what happened to Polycarp?
IRV: He refused to deny Christ . . . and was burned alive.
KID: Wow . . . When do things get better for these early Christians?
IRV: They already have. It's now 420 AD. Rome made Christianity a legal religion in the early 300s.
KID: So things were easy from then on?
IRV: Not exactly. That's why we're here in Hippo.
KID: You mean, we're in a hippopotamus?
IRV: No, Kid. Hippo is the name of this city. We're here to chat with a leader of

the early church. His name is Augustine, and if I'm not mistaken there he is. Augustine! Sir!

(Augustine enters from offstage right.)

AUGUSTINE: You called?

KID: Yes, sir. We came here hoping for a chance to talk with you.

IRV: My young friend here wonders if things are running smoothly for the Church, now that the Empire is no longer persecuting Christians.

AUGUSTINE: Things are easier. But there are still problems.

KID: Like what?

AUGUSTINE: Well, part of the reason the Empire has let up on persecution of anybody is that it's getting weaker. And some think that Christianity is causing the fall of the Roman Empire.

KID: You're kidding! Who thinks that?

AUGUSTINE: Unfortunately, a lot of people do! Some believe that the old Roman gods made the Empire strong. They think that when the Empire adopted Christianity, the old gods got angry and are destroying the Empire.

KID: What can you do?

AUGUSTINE: I'm glad you asked. I want to help clear up some misunderstandings about Christianity. For instance, Christians think that it's all right for them to make a living by begging. So I'm teaching about the importance of earning a living. And then, some think that joining the Church is just the thing to do, so I am teaching about being truly changed by Jesus Christ.

KID: But what can you do about the misunderstandings that people outside the Church have?

AUGUSTINE: In my book called *The City of God*, I tried to answer those who think that Christianity caused the Empire's problems. Their misunderstanding stems from our calling Jesus "Lord," instead of Caesar. Saying "Jesus is Lord" never meant that we were trying to overthrow any earthly government. A Christian should be a fine citizen of both God's Kingdom and an earthly country. But if forced to choose between them, the Christian must choose God's Kingdom, which will last forever.

KID: How can someone be a citizen of both kingdoms?

IRV: Thank you, sir! Time to go home.

(Augustine exits offstage left as lights flash off and on. Scenery should be same as the beginning when lights rest fully up.)

KID: Wow! How do you do that?

IRV: Don't ask . . . just enjoy it. They're holding dinner for you, Kid.

(Kid exits left. Irv says final line during his exit right:)

IRV: Let's see a digital watch match that . . . .

(CURTAIN)

AN OLD ST. BERNARD TEACHES NEW TRICKS

Cast:
Irv Inchworm
The Kid
Bowser—the Kid's St. Bernard Dog
Bernard
Bruno—the Village Ruffian

(Offstage sounds of a large dog barking and playful shouting of commands like "Go get it!" "That's it, fetch!" and "Good boy!" are heard. Kid enters from left.)

KID *(calling)*: Here, Bowser! Come on! Let's rest!

(Bowser enters from the left—the dog is obviously a St. Bernard and is panting.)

KID: Whew! Nearly wore each other out, didn't we?

(Irv Inchworm enters from right—his body is halfway onstage when he notices Bowser and stops short.)

IRV: Psst . . . hey, Kid! Did you feed your dog today?

KID: Irv! Good to see you! Oh, you mean Bowser? Don't worry about him.

IRV: Promise he won't step on me, either?

KID: Promise.

IRV *(moving closer to Kid and Bowser)*: Nice puppy. Say, he's a St. Bernard, right?

KID: You couldn't tell?

IRV: You know who these dogs are named after? Quite a guy, old Bernard. I'll bet your puppy here could tell the story if he had the chance. *(Bowser barks excitedly.)*

KID: Look, Irv, I appreciate your letting me talk to some Church fathers. I don't know how you did it, but— Bowser telling the story? Don't push it, Irv. Really, I mean . . .

IRV: I'm telling you, Kid. All it takes is imagination, information, and connections with the scriptwriter.

KID *(pause)*: Well . . . it would be kind of fun . . . .

(Lights flash on and off. Bowser barks excitedly: when lights cease flashing and are up, the scenery could show a mountain village. Bowser's barking leads into the following line:)

BOWSER: Rowlf! . . . Rowlf? . . . Really! *(Bowser has a cultured accent.)* I've been waiting for this chance for so long! *(to Kid)* Listen, about my feeding schedule . . .

IRV: Later, Rover. Look, we're in the Italian Alps. Village of Aosta. Don't waste the scenery. Give the Kid some background information, please.

BOWSER: Oh, all right. Bernard was born to a rich family in the year A.D. 923. His family didn't really want him to be a minister. It would mean that Bernard would have to give up a marriage his family had arranged for him.

KID: Being a minister wasn't such a bad deal back then,

35

was it!?
BOWSER (*clearing throat*): It also meant giving up some of his rights to the family fortune.
KID: Ohh . . .
BOWSER: Bernard was the head of the church in Aosta. This village had some rough characters in it . . . like this fellow coming toward us. (*Bowser motions to offstage right. Bruno enters from offstage right.*)
BOWSER: Good day, sir.
BRUNO: What's so good about it? Look around you! We're poor in this village, we are. We can barely scrape a living together, except what we can beg . . . or steal. . . . Say, you're dressed well, now aren't you, lad. Your clothes would fit my oldest child about right . . .
KID: My clothes . . . my clothes?
BRUNO: Oh, that's right. Wouldn't want to take your clothing, would we? You might freeze. But surely someone with your clothing would have a nice sum of money with him to keep those clothes nice. Hand it over!
BOWSER (*to audience*): I think I should do something here. Pardon me . . . (*Bowser growls threateningly. Bernard enters from offstage left.*)
BERNARD: What's the commotion here?
KID: I don't know who you are, but I must be glad to see you, too!
BERNARD: Oh, I'm Bernard of Menthon, the church leader of this village. I see you've met one of our citizens.
IRV: Not by name yet.
BERNARD: This is Bruno. By the way things look, I would guess that Bruno asked to share in your belongings.
KID: In a manner of speaking, you might say so.
BERNARD (*sighs*): Bruno, haven't we been trying our best to care for your family?
BRUNO: Yes, but these are strangers. They should know of our reputation. No one has made it through our village without leaving some kind of payment

36

since I can remember!

BERNARD: But leaving that payment of their own free will has been another matter, hasn't it? Bruno, don't you think Aosta deserves a better reputation? Our Lord Jesus said, "Whatever you did for one of the least of these brothers of mine, you did for me." I think we ought to show hospitality to travelers and other strangers among us, don't you?

BRUNO: But what if there isn't enough to care for those of us who live here?

BERNARD: Bruno, remember that you and your family were once strangers to me. Had I had the same attitude toward you then as you have toward travelers now, you would have received no help at all. But we were glad to help you, and we're still glad to help you. Our Lord will supply all our needs. *(pause)* Don't you think you owe our friends here an apology?

BRUNO: Well . . . I'm sorry I bothered you.

BERNARD: That's better. Walk with me for a while, Bruno. I have an idea I'd like to tell you. I'd like to build an aid station for travelers that come our way. . . .

(Bernard and Bruno exit left.)

KID: An aid station! What a great idea! Instead of travelers being afraid to come this way, they'd be glad to!

BOWSER: Bernard built his aid station, with the help of the villagers. The very people who had once robbed travelers and strangers were helping them, because Bernard had cared for the villagers. Bernard made it plain that the Gospel was to be practiced.

IRV: Travelers were so grateful, and the villagers so impressed by Bernard's example that two passes in the Swiss and Italian Alps were named after St. Bernard.

BOWSER: Not only that, but an exceptionally handsome type of mountain guide dog was named for Bernard. Known for loyalty and service, this breed of canine soon won the hearts of thousands throughout the . . .

IRV: Time to go home, Kid?
KID: Sounds that way, doesn't it?
BOWSER: Wait! I've got to talk to you about my feeding schedule! *(Lights flash on and off several times)*
BOWSER: Rowlf! . . . Rowlf?
KID: Irv, thanks again! Bowser, let's run outside for a while!
(Bowser whimpers, then exits left with kid.)

IRV: I always liked the Middle Ages . . . (to audience) . . . Hey, think about this one: When you need aid in the Swiss mountains, what do you say? *(pause)* Give up? You say, " 'Alp! 'Alp!" *(pause)* See, the mountains there are the Alps, so you call out . . . oh, well . . . never mind.

(Irv exits left.)

(CURTAIN)

BACK TO THE BASICS

Cast:
Irv Inchworm
The Kid
Martin Luther
Huldreich Zwingli
Teresa of Avila

(As sketch begins, Irv and The Kid are entering from the left side of the stage.)

IRV: Really an impressive game, Kid! Three hits out of four at bats!

KID: I had a good day. But coach says I need to learn to switch-hit. He's right. It'll make me a better all-around player. I might have gone four-for-four if I could switch-hit.

IRV: Maybe by next game?

KID *(laughs)*: Are you kidding? It's a long process. In some ways, it's like learning to hit all over again.

IRV: Back to the basics, huh?

KID: You might say so.

IRV: I just did. Speaking of which, how are the basics in your Christian life?

KID: What do you mean?

IRV: Let's compare it with learning to switch-hit. You want to be a more complete ballplayer, so you're learning to switch-hit, right?

KID: Right.

IRV: What if you tried to learn how to switch-hit and forgot the basics?

KID: I'd probably never learn how to switch-hit.

IRV: A lot of people have tried to be better Christians, but haven't gotten very far because they forgot the basics of wanting God to be first, praying often, reading the Bible, and living sincerely for God and others. In fact, there was a time when much of the Church was like that.

KID: Wow, that must have been a mess!

IRV: Sure was. But there were a few who remembered the basics and worked hard to remind others how important the basics were. They were called "Reformers" because they wanted to reform the Church. Hey, want to meet a few Reformers? You might pick up some pointers.

KID: Sure, but please tell me how you do it!

IRV: All it takes is imagination, information, and . . .

KID: *(cutting in to finish line)* I know . . . connections with the scriptwriter! . . . . Hey, I've been learning so much from these people I've met, I'd like to give them something. Think any of them need help on their swing?

IRV: Ah . . . well, Kid . . . tell you what, why don't you just enjoy this again?

(Lights flash on and off several times; then fully on. Scenery could suggest a Swiss village.)

KID: Switzerland? You know, we should have brought my St. Bernard.

IRV: We could have, but he wasn't around. Back to meeting a Reformer. This is Zurich. We're here to see Huldreich Zwingli in action. He'll probably offer some fine advice on the basics. To City Hall!

KID: City Hall ? Was Zwingli a mayor or something?

IRV: No, just a pastor who did what he could to live out his faith. Zwingli used his influence to secure freedom for others to preach the truth of Scripture. The City Council in Zurich respected Zwingli and what he had to say. Let's take a look.

(Kid and Irv exit right, then reappear left. Zwingli enters from offstage right.)

ZWINGLI: Gentlemen of the council: I know you seek to govern the city wisely. Toward that end, we must let the Scriptures tell us what we need to know about our lives and conduct. In order to do that, we must read and study the Scriptures.

KID *(aside to Irv)*: This is a city council meeting?

ZWINGLI: Also, we must compare how we act and what we say to the Scriptures. If our thoughts, our actions, our doctrine, our traditions, or our laws do not align with what Scripture says, then we must change them. You and I must lead our people in Christian conduct, gentlemen, according to the Scripture. Think on these things!

KID: Zwingli believes in Bible study, huh?

IRV: To put it mildly. But we're not done yet, Kid!

(Lights flash off and on several times, then remain on, scenery could reflect arid Spanish setting.)

KID: Quite a change in climate. Where are we now?

IRV: Spain, Kid.

KID: Awesome! I love tacos!

IRV: No, no, not Mexico. Spain. Zwingli did most of his reforming early in the sixteenth century. Now we'll meet someone who greatly influenced the latter portion of the sixteenth century.

KID: All right. Who is he?

IRV: Not "he," Kid, "she," Teresa of Avila. She was one of the reformers who tried reforming from within the official Roman Catholic Church. I mean really within. Right now we're inside a convent, so keep your voice down.

(Teresa enters from left, praying as she enters.)

TERESA: . . . and, Father, change our ways and thoughts to be more pleasing to You. Guide me, Lord. Amen.

IRV: Sister Teresa?

TERESA: Yes? How may I help you?

IRV: We're here to ask you about becoming a better Christian. What are some things that a person who really wants to grow as a Christian can do and should remember?

TERESA: Oh, how nice it is to hear someone who wants to know God more deeply! So few seem to really want to be a disciple of Jesus. One of the most important things is to use the privilege of prayer as often as possible. In order to know God's will, we must talk with Him. The Lord Jesus spent much time in prayer and we should, too. But so few really want to talk with God these days . . .

KID: Thanks for answering our questions. I'll remember to pray.

TERESA: God bless you!

(Teresa exits right as lights flash off and on. Lights stay fully on. Scenery could reflect a German village.)

IRV: Welcome to Wittenberg, Kid! We're going to meet Martin Luther. He'll probably have some great pointers on the basics, too.

(Sound effect: Hammer pounding several times, then stopping. Luther enters from right.)

KID: Are you Martin Luther?

(Luther stops.)

LUTHER: I am.

KID: Building something?

LUTHER: Eh? Oh, the hammer. No, I just tacked up some debate topics on the door of the Castle Church here in Wittenberg. There are some points on which I differ with the Church.

IRV: Would you mind telling us how you differ?

LUTHER: We cannot buy or work our way into Heaven, as many of the Church leaders seem to think. I have prayed and studied the Scriptures for years. Through this Scripture study and prayer, I came to understand that God loves me. He sent Jesus Christ to die for me that I might have eternal life. I can do nothing to receive this life, but have faith in God and commit my whole self to Him.

KID: That's great! There are the basics! Bible study, prayer, faith, commitment.

LUTHER: My, but you listen well!

IRV: Doesn't he, though? Thank you for your time, Dr. Luther. Say good-bye, Kid.

KID: Good-bye! And thanks!

(Luther exits as lights flash off and on. When lights are fully up, scenery should be same as beginning.)

IRV: You listen well, Kid. Remember the basics: Bible study, prayer, faith, and commitment.

KID: Right! And I'll work on those at least as much as I work on switch-hitting!

(Irv and The Kid begin to exit lift. Irv delivers last line as they exit.)

IRV: You know, Kid, you could be the first reformer with a .450 batting average!

(Irv and Kid complete exit.)

(CURTAIN)

THE GOSPEL GOING AND COMING

Cast:
Irv Inchworm
The Kid
John Wesley
Spangenberg
Jonathan Edwards

(As sketch opens, Kid enters from offstage left as he is saying opening lines:)

KID: Let's see—July 4, 1776 was the signing of the Declaration of Independence . . . the first Continental Congress was called in 1774 . . . the Quebec Act of 1774 . . . *(Irv's head appears just onstage right.)*

IRV: Psst . . . Kid . . . Hey, Kid!
KID: Irv!

(Irv makes full entrance from right while he says the next line.)

IRV: I heard so many facts and dates being thrown around, I thought I'd check in and see what's going on. So, what's going on?
KID: We're studying American history at school. I really like it, but there's a lot to remember.
IRV: Yeah, like, "Columbus sailed the ocean blue in

44

fourteen-hundred-ninety-two" and stuff . . .
KID: Actually, for this test we're not going back quite that far.
IRV: Have they said anything to you about "The Great Awakening"?
KID: Is that when Washington's troops caught the Hessians napping on Christmas night, 1776?
IRV: No . . . I'm talking about a spiritual revival that swept through the colonies during the eighteenth century!
KID: Oh, yeah. I think they have mentioned something about it.
IRV: Kid, it sounded to me like you were all set for the exam. Ready for a short break?
KID: Oh, boy! Are we going back to the Colonies?
IRV: Where else? Let's talk to a couple of men involved in the Awakening.
KID: Just imagination, information, and connections with the scriptwriter, right?
IRV: You're a fast learner.
(Lights flash off and on, then rest at fully on. Scenery could show an ocean dock in colonial Savannah, Georgia.)
KID: Mmm . . . smell that ocean air! Where are we?
IRV: Savannah, Georgia, spring, 1735. And while you're loving the ocean air, look at that guy.
(Irv and Kid look offstage right.)
KID: Wow! Does he ever look sick!! *(Wesley enters from offstage right.)* Who is it?
IRV: A young missionary from England. His name is John Wesley.
WESLEY: Now I know I'm ill! I thought I heard this worm speak!
KID: You did!
WESLEY: It was a stormy trip over. I was sick most of the time. I should expect to see things—but a talking worm?
KID: Sorry you had a bad trip.
WESLEY: Thank you for your concern, lad. It was hard, but in the end, it might turn out well.
KID: You sound as though you're still on your journey over.

WESLEY: In a sense, I am. You see, I met some special people on the ship. In the midst of the most violent storms on the way here, when many of the passengers and crew were afraid that the ship would sink, these people stayed calm. When I asked them why, they answered that their faith in Jesus Christ gave them peace. There I was, a missionary, and these Moravians—that's what they called themselves—were showing me a deeper faith than I'd ever seen. They told me that their leader here would talk to me about it.

IRV: Who's their leader?

WESLEY: He's a gentleman named Spangenberg.

(Spangenberg enters from offstage left.)

SPANGENBERG: Is one of you John Wesley?

IRV & KID *(turning toward Wesley)*: He is!

SPANGENBERG: Hello, I'm Spangenberg, of the Moravians. Some of the people who just arrived said you might wish to talk. Say, you look like you had a rough time of it!

WESLEY: Rough, indeed, but maybe worthwhile. Sir, I was astounded at how calm your people were when facing shipwreck on the way here. I'm a missionary for the Church of England. I'm familiar with the Gospel. But I still was terrified—yet your people were at peace.

SPANGENBERG: Yes, they knew they were safe in Christ, each of them. Tell me, do you know Jesus is your Savior?

WESLEY *(pause)*: I must think on this . . . I would like to hear more . . . .

(Wesley and Spangenberg exit left.)

KID: Wesley didn't look like he was ready to do much awakening, Irv. There must be more to tell.

IRV: You'd better believe it, Kid. Wesley finished his missionary tour in the Colonies and returned to England. He sought out a Moravian leader in London to

46

talk further. Wesley wanted the faith the Moravians had. In May of 1738, Wesley was listening to a reading of how Luther's faith had become real to him. While he listened, Wesley felt his own heart warmed, convincing him that God had indeed saved him because of his own trust in Christ. That night changed John Wesley. He traveled throughout the British Isles as a bold preacher of the Gospel and started new fellowships of Christians, stressing personal, inner knowledge of Christ as Savior.

KID: So how does all this connect with the revival in the Colonies?

IRV: Preachers from England established preaching circuits throughout the Colonies. Thousands of Colonists were awakened spiritually through those efforts. Because Wesley had been there before, he was able to wisely organize the missionary efforts.

KID: You might say that John Wesley went to the Colonies for his own awakening, and then saw to it that workers went there to awaken the Colonists!

IRV: Quite a mouthful—but right on the money, Kid. . . . We have one more stop to make. Hang on . . .

(Lights flash off and on several times, then stay fully on. Scenery could show colonial town in wooded area.)

KID: Where are we now?

IRV: Northampton, Massachusetts. Many people trace America's Great Awakening to this place, because of the preaching and teaching of Jonathan Edwards.

KID: One man? Who is this Jonathan Edwards guy, anyway?

(Edwards enters from offstage right, saying his first line under Irv's answer to the Kid.)

IRV: Over there—preaching in the churchyard.

(Irv and Kid turn toward Edwards.)

EDWARDS: I greet you today in the grace of the Lord

Jesus Christ, the love of God the Father, and the fellowship of the Holy Spirit. Amen. *(clears throat)* Many people trace this current revival back to Northampton because of things I've taught and said. That's very flattering, but all I've done is preach the truth of God. It is news to many that one must come to a personal relationship with God to be saved. For years, it seems that no one has told the truth that people must take responsibility for their decisions; they must repent, their response must be real and deep.

KID: I guess if I heard that message for the first time, it would wake me up!

IRV: No kidding, Kid! Well, let's head for home . . .

(Edwards exits right as lights flash off and on, resting at on.)

IRV: I'll let you get back to your studying now, Kid.

KID: Thanks, Irv. I learned a lot.

(Kid exits left.)

IRV: History's always been one of my favorite things. I really like the little rhymes to help you remember facts. Stick with you forever, you know? "Columbus sailed the ocean blue in fourteen-hundred-ninety-two." *(Irv starts to exit right, then stops midway.)* Or is it "Columbus sailed the deep blue sea in fourteen-hundred-ninety-three"? Hm, oh, well . . . . *(Irv shakes his head and completes exit.)*

(CURTAIN)

FABULOUS FORUMS
The Fabulous Forum on Prayer
by Jim Townsend, Ph.D.

Imagine what Biblical characters would say if they were interviewed by someone in your church. These two panel discussions, "Fabulous Forum on Prayer" and "Fabulous Forum on Faith and Works," can precede sermons on the topics of prayer and faith/works. They can also be used at retreats, club meetings, Sunday school classes, family nights, etc.

Assign parts to teens or adults who might read, memorize, or ad-lib their lines. Arrange chairs so that actors are seated in a semicircle in front of the audience. Dress Bible characters in simple bathrobes and sandals. The moderator can wear a suit or other contemporary clothing.

Cast:
Skip Tick—moderator
Hannah
David
Paul
James

SKIP TICK, MODERATOR: Hi, I'm Skip Tick, your razzle-dazzle moderator for today's fabulous forum. You'll pardon me if I seem a little skip-tick-al, or, I mean skeptical about our subject of discussion today: "Does prayer have anything to do with real problems?" Well, we're going to sift through our four panelists' claims. These folks have been flown to our forum straight out of Bible times. Let's welcome Hannah, David, Paul, and James.

HANNAH: Thanks, Skip.

JAMES: It's great to be here.

DAVID: Though it was a long flight.

SKIP: Well, let's get started. I say that prayer is nice for church mice, pastors, and hermits. But I have to live in the hard knocks, commuter-and-computer world. Are you going to convince me that prayer works in the world of study halls and video games?

HANNAH: Prayer sure made a difference in my life. I got about ten pounds, six ounces worth of answered prayer! He got diapered, and his name was Samuel. Before that, I'd been made fun of for having no children. In my day, that was tragic.

SKIP: But how do you know there was any real cause-and-effect connection, Hannah, between your praying and having the baby you wanted? Maybe it was just wishful thinking, or real positive thinking.

HANNAH: I think you'd be pretty convinced after being laughed at behind your back for months. My enemy kept provoking me about it until I got provoked at God. I was so upset that I was starving myself. I was as skeptical as you, Skip. But getting results from prayer makes believers out of people. God answered me directly, with a yes.

SKIP: Are you going to tell me that if I pray to God, I'll get anything I want? That sounds like quite a heavenly candy machine to me.

JAMES: No, Skip, we wouldn't put it that way. In fact, once I told some Christians that they weren't getting what they wanted from God because of why they wanted it. Prayer isn't just getting the gimmes. God's no pushover grandfather who'll give you a lot of junk you shouldn't have.

He is a good Father who gives His children what's best for them.

SKIP: So you're saying that sometimes God denies your requests. I think I see two possibilities emerging—your God answers yes or no.

PAUL: If you want to add another possibility, Skip, here's a third one. God sometimes answers differently than you expected. In other words, He says, "Surprise!" Take my "thorn in the flesh." Was that thing ever bugging me! I wanted to ditch it, for sure. So I checked it out with God in prayer. But I didn't get any candy-machine, instant answer. Instead, I was told that God's grace would help me put up with my "thorn." He would give me what I needed to cope with it.

SKIP: Can you tell us more about this type of answer?

PAUL: Most of the time we want to be rid of problems. But sometimes they're like an irritating grain of sand that gets inside an oyster shell. The oyster puts up with its irritation for so long that someday someone opens the oyster—only to find a pearl inside.

SKIP: In other words, Paul, you're saying that people's problems can be pearls in disguise, if they handle them with the right kind of attitude.

PAUL: That's right. Prayer's not a cop-out; instead, it can be a cope-with-it mechanism. God chooses to handle our problems differently than the way we might choose to handle them.

SKIP: Looks like you people have three types of prayer answers going here: yes, no, and surprise.

DAVID: Let's make it four ways. Sometimes God delays to answer when we present our problems to Him in prayer. He says, "Wait." I remember when all my family was taken hostage—along with the families of all our soldiers—at a place called Ziklag. The troops were about to turn into a lynch mob on me, but I sought God's help and encouragement.

SKIP: And did prayer work in your case, David?

DAVID: Yes, but it worked in the way a fuse is connected to a stick of dynamite. There was a delayed reaction before the positive results came. In fact, you might say that we were the answer to our own prayer, because we had to go retrieve our families from the enemy—once God had shown us through an Egyptian where they were held hostage.

JAMES: Sure enough. Because God sometimes delays, I had to tell some Christians once that just as a farmer has to wait for a crop to grow, so we have to be patient in our waiting.

PAUL: Yes, I, too, had to tell Christians to "pray without ceasing." That doesn't mean that you have to pray every second of the day and night. It's like having a cough. That little nagging irritation just keeps coming back, so that you cough and cough and cough. You might say that you have a chronic cough. Even so, God wants chronic prayers.

SKIP: Whew! After all that, I don't think I can still be skeptical about the way prayer helps us with personal problems. Let's wrap up our forum. You've given four ways God ties in prayer to problems:

1. He may say, "Yes."
2. He may say, "No."
3. He may even say, "Surprise!"
4. He may say, "Wait."

This is Skip Tick signing off until tomorrow. I'll be praying!

The Fabulous Forum on Faith and Works
by Kent Lindberg

Cast:
Faye Anne Werks—moderator
Paul
James
Mr. H.—writer of Hebrews

FAYE: Hi, Faye Anne Werks here, your faithful, friendly moderator for an insightful discussion with our panel of experts. Today, our discussion centers on the relationship between faith and works. For the past two centuries, Christians have verbally battled over which one is more important. To help us with today's topic, I've invited three Bible personalities to populate our panel. Folks, please welcome Paul, James, and our mystery writer of Hebrews. *(Mystery writer has mask on. Faye stares at him a moment, as do the others.)* Excuse me, mystery writer of Hebrews, but what's with the mask? Are you having an identity crisis?

MR. H.: No, Faye. I know my identity, as did the original readers of my book, but I'm kinda shy. I guess I like my privacy.

FAYE: We try to respect the privacy of every guest panelist. Would it would be all right to call you Mr. H.?

MR. H.: Sure, Faye.

FAYE: Okay, panel, let's get into our controversy. Many theologians who spend their time meditating on the Book of Romans seem to stress faith. Christians who hand out tracts, mow the church lawn, and sing in the choir seem to push works. So what's the relationship between the two? Is faith more important than works, or are works more important than faith?

MR. H.: May I start? As you recall from my Book of Hebrews, faith is the assurance of things we hope for, such as eternal life. Even though we can't see eternal life, we know that it is real.

FAYE: That sounds kinda cosmic, Mr. H. Can you define faith in more earthly terms?

MR. H.: Let's see. Suppose your trusted friend gave you the title to your dream home. But you can't move into the house for several years. You know you own the place, but your residency there is based on a promise. For Christians, Jesus is that trusted friend who promises us an eternal future.

PAUL: As Mr. H. says, faith involves us in an ongoing friendship with Jesus—the Christ. Actually He's more than a friend. He's like a hero who has saved us from death. All we need to do is believe that He has saved us.

FAYE: But don't we need to do something with our faith in Jesus? It seems that a lot of churches write a faith statement in the church constitution and reaffirm it at annual meetings. This kind of faith reminds me of moldy prayer books.

JAMES: Faith needs to be active here and now. This is where works come in.

FAYE: What do you mean by works, James? Is that something like asking for the "works" when you order a big, deluxe hamburger?

JAMES: No, Faye, although

I could go for a quarter pounder right now. Works can be described as those Christian actions done in love. They result from our faith in Jesus Christ.

FAYE: Are you saying that a Christian who doesn't act out his faith to others possesses a dead faith?

JAMES: You sure know your stuff, Faye. A dead faith involves no real commitment to God. It's like serving God leftovers.

FAYE: But Paul has written that faith is more important than works. The issue for him is faith. He doesn't worry about works as evidence of a vibrant faith. Doesn't Paul contradict you, James?

JAMES: Not really, Faye. But I'll let Paul explain.

PAUL: Thanks, James. In my writings to the Roman believers, I stressed the importance of faith over works. I was reacting to Jews who based their faith only upon works. Their "dos and don'ts" were numerous and strictly enforced, but they hated Christ, God's Son. They used to get furious when Jesus broke a Sabbath rule, but they were blind to His holiness. I was the same way before I encountered Christ on the road to Damascus. I thought, how could these guys disobey the Jewish laws and say they love God? Now, I know that my petty rituals were empty since I did not have faith in God's Son as Lord and Savior.

FAYE: So you, Paul, want your readers to understand that a relationship with Christ is imperative?

PAUL: That's correct, Faye. Our security in being a child of God is not based on how many church committees, potluck dinners, or even prayer meetings we attend. Our security begins with faith. We must believe in Christ as Savior and Lord. Works are a natural result of our faith, a visible confirmation of it. In my Book of Romans, I challenged those religious Jews who used works to make themselves right before

God. Our works just aren't good enough.

JAMES: In my writings, I was correcting the so-called believers who said that they had faith in Christ yet did not act like Him. So I challenged these people to show their faith through their works. Christianity is action, Faye. In fact, an entire book of the Bible is named Acts.

FAYE: Then where is the balance between faith and works?

PAUL: Both faith and works are necessary. However, works alone are not what Christ desires from us. Through our faith, we know that Jesus has made us presentable in God's eyes.

JAMES: And a faith with no visible signs of action reflects an empty faith. It's like attempting to drive a Corvette Stingray without the motor. Take Sunday-morning-only Christians, for example. They act out their faith once a week for an hour. Besides that visit to the church, there's no Bible study, no evangelism, no food for the hungry, no emotional or financial aid to widows and orphans. Believers who do nothing have fallen flat on their faith.

FAYE: I like the way you put it, James. So there's a balance between the two. How about an example of a believer who had faith, and then acted on it?

MR. H.: Toward the end of my book, I shared how people in the Old Testament proved their faith.

FAYE: Is that the section where most of the paragraphs begin with the word "by"?

MR. H.: I see that you're familiar with my writings. People like Abel, Noah, Abraham, Joseph, Rahab, and Gideon acted out their faith in pretty precarious situations.

FAYE: Like when Abraham offered up Isaac as a sacrifice to God?

MR. H.: Now there's a great action scene, Faye. Here's faithful Abe making preparations to sacrifice his only son. Without faith in his God, Abe's attempted sacrifice would have been horrible. And without action, Abe's faith would been only empty words.

JAMES: I stressed the way Abraham's faith and actions worked together. Abe's faith was strengthened by what he did to please God.

PAUL: In my writings, I stressed Abraham's righteousness that came about through his faith in God's promises. How was his faith visible? By his willingness to sacrifice his only heir.

FAYE: I see. Let's see if we can summarize.

1. James has pointed out that faith without works is a dead faith. We need to act on our faith.

2. And Paul has pointed out that works alone cannot make us right before God. Faith is the door by which we enter our relationship with the Lord. The natural result of that relationship is works.

3. And Abraham is a good example of someone who believed God and put his faith into action.

Remember then, not only to keep the faith, but also act on it. Faith and works go hand in hand. James, speaking of works, let's get some quarter pounders.

IN THE BEGINNING
A Scripture-based Choral Reading
Celebrating God's Creation
by David and Becca Toht

This action choral reading, written especially for elementary children, might be used for an entire Sunday school or worship hour. No special props or costumes are needed.

Interpretive Sound and Movement

In advance, experiment with different ways of presenting the reading. Children enjoy interpretive movement. Practice with them until they perform the motions smoothly.

Decide whether voices will rise or fall at the end of a line. Underline words that will be stressed. Mark the lines that will be read softly, slowly, loudly, etc. Try to present the reading the same way each time you practice it. Teach children to enunciate clearly, especially final consonants. You'll need a cue for starting. You might say, "One, two, three!" or "Ready, start!"

You might use cue cards or charts so that the children can read their parts instead of memorizing them. You might also give copies of the entire script to an older child who can follow along and cue those who forget their parts.

Cast:
Chorus 1
Chorus 2
Narrator 1
Narrator 2
Solo 1 and 2 (*can use different children each time*)

The First Day
Sing "This Is My Father's World."

	Interpretive Movement

ALL: In the beginning, God created.

NARRATOR 1: The earth was dark and as bare as a ball of clay. An icy cold wind blew without stopping.

NARRATOR 2: Not a bird chirped. No leaves rustled. Not a waterfall splashed. All was silent and empty.

(pause)

Students stand in a row or semicircle, their arms outstretched facing audience, hands and heads down.

Raise arms, fingers spread, faces up, smiling.

SOLO 1: Then God said, "Let there be light." And the earth was bathed in golden light.

SOLO 2: The light was warm and full of life. Where there was nothing at all, God had made something!

ALL: Let us praise the great Creator!

CHORUS 1: God was pleased with what He made.

CHORUS 2: There was day and night—the first day.

Lower hands to each others' shoulders. (This chorus movement will be repeated periodically.)

The Second Day

ALL: In the beginning, God created.

NARRATOR 1: God said, "There will be clouds in the sky and oceans on the earth."

NARRATOR 2: And so on the second day, He made blue sky. The clouds moved slowly in the sky like huge white mountains.

SOLO 1: Lord, how beautiful is Your creation!

SOLO 2: How wonderful is Your world!

ALL: Lord, You have made so many things. How wisely You have made them!

CHORUS 1: God was pleased with what He made.

CHORUS 2: There was day and night—the second day.

Chorus 1 raise arms and sway back and forth. Chorus 2 make wave motions with hands.

The Third Day

Sing "For the Beauty of the Earth."

ALL: In the beginning, God created.

NARRATOR 1: On the third day God pulled dry land from the bottom of the sea and arranged it as it pleased Him.

(Repeat hands-on-shoulders movement.)

Chorus 1 mimic molding mountains. Chorus 2 mimic scooping out valleys.

NARRATOR 2: He pushed mountains up from the depths of the earth and scooped out valleys.

SOLO 1: He let the waves of the waters dig out harbors and coves. He called the waters "seas."

SOLO 2: No place looked exactly the same as another.

CHORUS 1: He rules over the deserts and jungles.

CHORUS 2: He rules over the high mountains and sandy seashores.

ALL: Let us praise the great Creator!

NARRATOR 1: God commanded all sorts of plants and trees to grow on the land, and they sprang up to His glory.

NARRATOR 2: Bright colors splashed across the fields and mountains. Sweet fragrances drifted in the breeze.

SOLO 1: God made bluebells, snow white daisies, and sunny meadows of sweet clover.

SOLO 2: Waving pines and swinging vines—there was green the world over.

(Repeat hands-on-shoulders movement.)

All students squat down. Chorus 1 shoot up quickly, arms up, and sway. Chorus 2 "grow" slowly, wiggling fingers around hands.

CHORUS 1: God was pleased with what He made.
CHORUS 2: There was day and night—the third day.

(Repeat hands-on-shoulders movement.)

The Fourth Day

ALL: In the beginning, God created.
NARRATOR 1: God created lights to mark day and night, and to signal the seasons.

Raise arms over head in a circle.

NARRATOR 2: The greater light, the sun, ruled the day. The smaller light, the moon, ruled the night.
NARRATOR 1: Then God scattered the stars across the sky.

Raise hands and wave them, wiggling fingers a twinkling fashion.

NARRATOR 2: He set the planets in their courses.
SOLO 1: Praise Him, sun and moon!
SOLO 2: Praise Him, shining stars!
ALL: Praise Him, highest heavens!
CHORUS 1: God was pleased with what He made.
CHORUS 2: There was day and night—the fourth day.

(Repeat hands-on-shoulders movement.)

The Fifth Day

ALL: In the beginning, God created.

NARRATOR 1: Churning the waters of the oceans, God created sea creatures, saying,

SOLO 1: "Let the seas teem with fish—porpoise and whales, sea urchins and snails
—all things that live under the water."

SOLO 2: "Let the air come alive with birds."

NARRATOR 2: To the creatures of the sea and sky God said,

SOLO 1: "Have babies! Increase your numbers!"

SOLO 2: "Fill the ocean and sky with baby creatures just like you!"

CHORUS 1: Lord, how beautiful is Your creation!

CHORUS 2: How wonderful is Your world!

ALL: Lord, You have made so many things. How wisely You have made them!

CHORUS 1: God was pleased with what He made.

CHORUS 2: There was day and night—the fifth day.

Chorus 1 clasp hands together to make a fish shape and pretend the fish are jumping over waves. Chorus 2 flap hands like birds.

(Repeat hands-on-shoulders movement.)

The Sixth Day

Sing "All Things Bright and Beautiful."

ALL: In the beginning, God created.

NARRATOR 1: Turning to the land, God said, "From the earth let wild animals and livestock be created."

NARRATOR 2: "May each lead his life in his own way and in his own place."

SOLO 1: God made tortoises, tigers, turtles, and tree frogs; giraffes, gnu, geese, and groundhogs.

SOLO 2: Butterflies and buffalo, badgers, and beagles: antelope, elephants, egrets, and eagles.

CHORUS 1: He rules over the creatures that creep and slither.

CHORUS 2: He rules over the creatures that leap and run.

ALL: Let us praise the great Creator!

NARRATOR 1: God said, "Let us make people in our image, to be responsible for the fish, the fowl, and the animals." So God made man and woman.

Students silently act out different animals—cows lumbering, birds flapping their wings, elephants with long trunks swaying, rabbits hopping, slow turtles creeping around, etc.

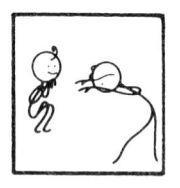

(Repeat hands-on-shoulders movement.)

Bow heads, arms at sides. Slowly "come alive," lifting heads and raising arms to the sky.

SOLO 1: Praise the Lord, for we are His people!

SOLO 2: Praise the Lord, for He has made us like unto Himself!

ALL: Let us praise the great Creator!

NARRATOR 2: God told the people every plant would be theirs for food.

SOLO 1: God gave them tomatoes and potatoes, turnips, tangerines; broccoli, beets, bananas, and beans.

SOLO 2: Sweet corn, squash, spinach, and cherries; peanuts, parsnips, and all kinds of berries.

CHORUS 1: God was pleased with what He made.

CHORUS 2: There was day and night—the sixth day.

Stretch arms up, pretending to pick fruit from bushes and trees and eat it.

(Repeat hands-on-shoulders movement.)

The Seventh Day

ALL: In the beginning, God created.

NARRATOR 1: And in the peace of the last day of creation God rested. His great work was finished.

NARRATOR 2: He looked with pleasure on all He had made.

Slowly kneel, placing hands together at side of head as though "sleeping."

ALL: And all was very, very good.

SOLO 1: God blessed the seventh day, making it holy.

SOLO 2: Because on it He rested from His work of creation.

CHORUS 1: Let us sing for joy to God!

CHORUS 2: Let us kneel before our Maker!

ALL: Let us praise the great Creator!

(Sing "Let the Whole Creation Cry.")

Remain kneeling. Place arms on each other's shoulders, smiling.

Chorus 1 leaps up, hands in the air. Then Chorus 2 does the same.

Chorus, narrators, and soloists come together in front and hold hands to sing final song.

This Is My Father's World

Maltbie D. Babcock
Franklin L. Sheppard

1. This is my Father's world, And to my list'ning ears All nature sings, and round me rings The music of the spheres. This is my Father's world; I rest me in the thought Of rocks and trees, of skies and seas; His hand the wonders wrought.

2. This is my Father's world; The birds their carols raise; The morning light, the lily white, Declare their maker's praise. This is my Father's world; Why should my heart be sad? The Lord is king, let the heavens ring; God reigns, let the earth be glad!

For the Beauty Of the Earth

Folliott S. Pierpoint
Conrad Kocher

1. For the beau-ty of the earth, For the glo-ry of the skies,
2. For the won-der of each hour Of the day and of the night,

For the love which from our birth O-ver and a-round us lies:
Hill and vale and tree and flower, Sun and moon and stars of light:

Lord of all, to Thee we raise This our hymn of grate-ful praise.

All Things Bright and Beautiful

Cecil F. Alexander
Traditional English melody

(Ref.) All things bright and beau-ti-ful, All crea-tures great and small,
All things wise and won-der-ful; The Lord God made them all. *Fine*

1. Each lit-tle flow'r that o-pens, Each lit-tle bird that sings,
2. The pur-ple head-ed moun-tain, The riv-er run-ning by,
3. The cold wind in the win-ter, The pleas-ant sum-mer sun,
4. He gave us eyes to see them, And lips that we might tell

D.C. Refrain

He made their glow-ing col-ors, He made their ti-ny wings.
The sun-set, and the morn-ing That bright-ens up the sky.
The ripe fruits in the gar-den: He made them, ev-ery one.
How great is God Al-might-y, Who has made all things well.

69

Let the Whole Creation Cry

Christoph Anton

1. Let the whole cre-a-tion cry, "Glo-ry to the Lord on high!"
   Heav'n and earth, a-wake and sing, "Praise him, our al-might-y King!"
   Praise him, star-ry skies a-bove, Tell of our Cre-a-tor's love;
   Sun and moon, lift up your voice; Night and day in God re-joice.

2. Crea-tures large and crea-tures small, Praise your Cre-a-tor, one and all!
   Ea-gles soar-ing in the sky, Dol-phins leap-ing in re-ply.
   Roo-sters crow-ing at the dawn, Grace-ful deer and trem-bling fawn.
   All of these to God be-long; Let them join cre-a-tion's song.

3. Men and wom-en, young and old, Shout your prai-ses loud and bold,
   And let all with hap-py hearts In this wor-ship take their parts;
   God's cre-a-tion ev-ery-where, Let your prai-ses fill the air:
   "Ho-ly, Ho-ly, Ho-ly One; Glo-ry be to God a-lone!"

IF WE HAD BEEN THERE

An Easter Choral Reading
by Marilee Zdenek
adapted by Ramona Warren
A drama for four teens and a choir or soloist and guitar.

The four speakers should stand in various places on the stage. They should have their backs to the audience. The choir or soloist should be to one side of the speakers or at the back of the room. (Each speaker turns to face the audience as he/she speaks lines.)

Cast:
Choir or Soloist
Speakers *(four)*

1st SPEAKER: If we had been Jews, would we have spoken out for Him when the Sanhedrin accused Him of blasphemy?

2nd SPEAKER: If we had been Gentiles, would we have defended Him when the Romans condemned Him to death?

3rd SPEAKER: If we had been disciples, would we have stayed with Him when the crowd became a crucifying mob?

4th SPEAKER: Or would we have been like Peter—who followed Him and loved Him and denied Him three times before the dawn?

CHOIR OR SOLOIST: Were you there when they crucified my Lord? O! Sometimes it causes me to tremble, tremble, tremble.

1st SPEAKER: And the Christ who was crucified there, once said: "As you have done it to the least of these, My brothers, you have done it unto Me."

2nd SPEAKER: As nations rise in war,

3rd SPEAKER: As governments oppress the poor,

4th SPEAKER: As passive people turn and look aside,

(Speakers look at one another as they say the following lines in unison.)

ALL: In silence
We crucify.
Again—
We crucify.

(Speakers look at audience.)

1st SPEAKER: As indifference forms the pattern of our lives,

2nd SPEAKER: as hungry children cry for food,

3rd SPEAKER: as widows mourn alone in empty rooms,

(Speakers look at one another as they say the following lines in unison.)

ALL: In apathy—
We crucify.
Again—
We crucify.

CHOIR OR SOLOIST: Were you there when they nailed Him to the tree? O! Sometimes it causes me to tremble, tremble, tremble.

(Speakers turn away from one another and half away from audience as they speak. They should end their lines with their heads down.)

1st SPEAKER: I think of the nails that crucified my Lord.

2nd SPEAKER: They were made of iron; but more—

3rd SPEAKER: They were made of hatred, prejudice and greed.

4th SPEAKER: And I wonder—

1st SPEAKER: What part of myself is found in the shadow of that mob that stretches down through history?

2nd SPEAKER: What part of myself creates nails in other

forms that wound my brother—and my Lord?

3rd SPEAKER: You know how many times I have betrayed You, Lord.

4th SPEAKER: You know the times I have chosen evil over good.

ALL SPEAKERS: Guilt lies upon me like an iron cloak. My soul is heavy—my burden hard.

CHOIR OR SOLOIST: Were you there when He rose up from the grave? O! Sometimes it causes me to tremble, tremble, tremble.

(Speakers face audience again as they say their lines. They should begin with a tone of wonder and go on with growing excitement to joy. The speakers might raise their arms on the last line.)

1st SPEAKER: In the act of death, He absorbs our sins.

2nd SPEAKER: In love, He forgives our failures.

3rd SPEAKER: In the act of resurrection, He gives the promise of acceptance,

4th SPEAKER: the assurance of forgiveness,

1st SPEAKER: the affirmation of eternal life.

2nd SPEAKER: "Your sins are forgiven you," He said. "Go and sin no more."

3rd SPEAKER: Through Your love, I am made whole.

4th SPEAKER: Through Your death, I have found new life.

1st SPEAKER: You are my shield, my redeemer, and my hope.

ALL SPEAKERS: My sins are forgiven—Hallelujah!

Adapted from "If We Had Been There," a reading by Marilee Zdenek, in *Hymns for the Family of God*, © 1976 Paragon Associates, Inc., by permission of the author.

ON DEATH ROW
THE TRUE STORY OF DARLENE DEIBLER
AS TOLD TO KAREN BURTON MAINS

This play, written for teens or adults, reveals the power of God to sustain in even the worst circumstances.

The setting: The Island of Celebes in the Dutch East Indies, now Indonesia, at Japanese prisoner-of-war camps during World War II (1942 through 1945).

Props:
One wooden chair, stage center back. Manila folders to hold scripts for Readers and Chorus.

Directions:
Most parts are read rather than memorized. Most of the dramatic action is explained by the Chorus through chants. The stage is divided into four basic areas—stage right, stage left, stage center back, and stage center front.

Cast:
Man 1
Man 2
Woman 1
Woman 2
Darlene Deibler

All parts are read except Darlene's. Stage center back represents the Kempetai Prison. Stage center front is used when she is leaving Celebes.

COSTUMES:

Costumes are optional. Women, Darlene, and Chorus can wear tattered prisoner-of-war garb with few touches of the South China Seas—collie hats, mandarin collars. The men can wear drab shirts and pants. Men should slip on black armbands when they play Japanese officer roles.

(Play begins with Chorus at stage right. Man 1, Darlene (one step in front), and Man 2 at stage left.)

VOICE *(reads loudly from Chorus)*: This is Manila Radio broadcasting. Bombs are falling all around. This will be our last broadcast. I'm going to have to close down. *(pause)* COME ON, AMERICA!!

MAN 1: We huddled silently around our little radio and listened to the sob in that man's voice. It was 1942—the Philippines had fallen. Soon our island, Celebes, would be overrun. It would go as the others had before it—the Philippines, Singapore, the Malay Peninsula, Hong Kong.

MAN 2: Three men and six women were on our missionary staff. *(motions to Man 1)* Dr. Jaffray, our field chairman—a man in his seventies—and I, Russell Deibler, decided to take refuge from the enemy soldiers in the mountains at a retreat center belonging to the mission. We prayed it would provide our staff with shelter in this storm of World War II.

DARLENE: My husband, Russell *(motions to man 2)*, and I had come to the mission field of the South China Sea three years before on our very first wedding anniversary.

MAN 1: We had all come to these South China Seas to tell people about Christ.

CHORUS *(Marching feet. Each one shouting one of the following phrases.)*: All the men! Back of the truck! Step along! The men! The men!

75

(*one voice*) Leave that old man! He's so sick, he'll die anyway!

DARLENE: The Japanese came to our mission retreat. All the men except for Dr. Jaffray were loaded into the back of the truck. I ran, frantic, with a pillowcase filled with Russell's things and held them up to him. He leaned over and whispered, "Remember, dear. He said He would never leave or forsake us." The truck jerked away, and that's the last I ever saw of him.

(*Darlene bows head slightly. Man 2 turns back to audience.*)

MAN 1: We were under house arrest for a year. Native Christians smuggled food to us despite the penalty of death if they were caught by the soldiers.
(*Chorus makes sound of marching feet.*)

DARLENE: Finally we were transported to Kempeli, a concentration camp for fifteen hundred women and children. We were housed in twelve long barracks. Dr. Jaffray was taken to Paripari, the men's camp. His last words to me were, "Lassie, be a good soldier for Jesus Christ."

CHORUS (*keeps feet marching till end of this chant*): Be a soldier for Jesus Christ.
Be a soldier for Jesus Christ.
Be a soldier for Jesus Christ.
For Jesus Christ, for Jesus Christ.

DARLENE: Our forced labor began on that very day and continued through the remaining three years of war.

CHORUS: Feed the pigs. Dig the roads. Plant the crops. Carry loads. Chop down trees. Knit the socks. Toil in mud. Break the rocks. Uniforms. Sewing room. Wash the sties.

(*During this chant, two women step from Chorus* [*stage left*] *and walk across to join Darlene* [*stage right*]. *They stand in front of Menwho slip armbands onto sleeves.*)

DARLENE: Our first prison camp was located between

two Japanese airplane landing strips. The Allies began to bomb these by night.

WOMAN 1: We were ordered to dig slit trenches and lie in them during the bombings often in the cold monsoon rainstorms.

DARLENE: The first time we huddled in those trenches, with the sound of bombs whistling and exploding and the yak-yak of answering antiaircraft fire, the Lord spoke a word of promise to my heart.

CHORUS: It shall not come nigh thee. Psalm 91:7, A thousand shall fall at thy side, and ten thousand at thy right hand; but it shall not come nigh thee.

WOMAN 2: Our daily diet consisted of rice porridge with an occasional vegetable from the officers' garden. We promised we wouldn't talk to each other about food—but we couldn't help it.

DARLENE: When I get home, I'm going to have all the chocolate-covered cherries I can eat.

WOMAN 1: I'm going to have oranges, turkey with dressing, radishes.

CHORUS: Pumpkin pie, and roast beef, strawberries, lots to eat. Lots to eat! Lots to eat! Eat! Eat! Eat!

DARLENE: The toilets in the camp were so unsanitary—just open pits. With the pigs we had flies, and the flies spread the filth from the toilets and soon we had dysentery.

WOMAN 2: Within a few months, one-third of the camp—500 people—were dying with dysentery.

WOMAN 1: We had a siege of gastroenteritis. In two weeks all the infants in camp had died.

WOMAN 2: Women and children began to lose their minds. Little huts were erected at the end of camp for them and the doors were locked.

DARLENE: Sometimes, mad dogs would jump the barbed wire and attack the women as they huddled from the bombings in the trenches. We lost more to the dogs than we ever lost to the bombings.

WOMAN 1: Because our diet was so poor, we began to suffer from vitamin deficiency. There were sores that refused to heal, night blindness, and skin rashes.

DARLENE: Our work quotas continued. Some of us did two, three jobs a day to take the places of those who were ill.

WOMAN 2: And every night, after these long and horrible days, Darlene Deibler would call the women and children of her barracks to the front where they would gather for prayer and Bible reading. The peace and love in that place were unexplainable.

WOMAN 1: I had been given the responsibility of overseeing the women in that camp. I took orders from the camp commander, Mr. Yamagi, a man with an indescribable temper. Mrs. Deibler was a barracks' head—so we worked closely together—and she was such a dear. Though only in her early twenties, she maintained such a positive spirit—I suppose it was her faith. Then one day I was asked to take terrible news to Darlene Deibler.

DARLENE: Mrs. Youstraw came and asked if I had a moment. We walked to the front of the barracks and she said, "I have sad news. Your husband in the men's camp at Pari-pari has been very ill." I looked at her face, and when I saw the tears in her eyes I cried, "Oh, Mrs. Youstraw, you don't mean to say he's gone!"

WOMAN 1: It just broke my heart. This was November. He had died three months before, in August, but we had been forbidden to tell her.

DARLENE: It was one of those moments. I looked up into the face of my God and I cried, "Why! Why, God, why?" Don't let anyone ever tell you you can't ask why. Jesus did when He was on the Cross, and He was never so human as when He cried, "My God, my God, why—?" Then I heard His voice answering me so sweetly.

CHORUS: Yea, when thou passest through the waters, I will be with thee; and through the rivers, they shall not overflow thee.

MAN 1 *(turns around, calls)*: Darlene Deibler! Report to the Camp Commander's office!

MAN 2 *(turns also)*: Mrs. Deibler. I want to talk with you. This is war for everyone.

DARLENE: Yes, sir, Mr. Yamagi.

MAN 2: Women in Japan have also heard news like you've heard today.

DARLENE: Yes, yes, Mr. Yamagi. I understand that.

MAN 2: I just ask of you, don't lose your smile. You've been such a tremendous help to the other women in the camp. You're so young. When this war is finally over, you can go back to America. You can marry again and forget these awful days.

DARLENE: Mr. Yamagi— May I have permission to speak to you? *(He nods.)* I want to tell you about Somebody who has given me the hope that keeps me smiling. Maybe you've never heard about Him, but I learned about Him when I was a little girl in Sunday school. His name is Jesus, the Son of the Almighty God, the Creator of Heaven and earth.

And He gives those who follow Him love, love that circles the whole world. That's why I don't hate you, Sir. I don't hate the Japanese. I love you. I want you to know my God. *(Man turns back to audience.)*

Mr. Yamagi nodded and tears ran down his cheeks. Abruptly he went into his room, closed the door. But I knew he was weeping—I could hear him blowing his nose. After a while, although he hadn't dismissed me, I left.

WOMAN 1: The long black limousine of the Japanese Secret Service Police often pulled into camp. Women were taken. Some never came back. The ones who did never spoke of their experience.

WOMAN 2: Two of the

women missionaries were taken, women in their forties.

DARLENE: One day when that limousine came, I knew it had come for me—

MAN 1: Darlene Deibler!

CHORUS *(softly)*: Spy, spy, spy, spy. *(continues until Darlene, escorted by Men 1 & 2 on either side, reaches center stage back)*

WOMAN 2: Six months after learning of her husband's death, Darlene Deibler was accused of being an American spy and taken to the prison in the capital city of Macassar.

DARLENE: When the long black car pulled to a stop in front of the former insane asylum of Macassar, my heart cried, "Oh, Lord, You took Russell from me. Must I now go through this?"

CHORUS *(have two voice this softly)*: Whom the Lord loveth He chasteneth. *(Marching softly, whole chorus chants.)* Be a soldier for Jesus. A good soldier for Jesus Christ. A good, a good, a good soldier for Jesus Christ.

DARLENE: The guard took me to the boarded cell. On the door, written in Japanese, were the words—This Person Must Die. I knew I was on the death row. When that door shut, I sank to my knees and watched the key turn in the lock. Then in my heart there rose a song I learned as a child.

(Darlene drops to her knees, head bowed, lifts head when Chorus ends.)

CHORUS *(softly)*: Fear not, little flock, whatever your lot. He enters all rooms, the doors being shut. He never forsakes. He never is gone. So count on His Presence from darkness 'til dawn.

DARLENE: I knew they could shut me in, but they couldn't shut my God out.

MAN 1: Food! *(Man 2 turns back to audience. A man stands on either side of Darlene.)*

WOMAN 1 *(Darlene on knees pantomimes this reading.)*: A bowl of rice porridge, filled with stones, chaff, and worms. Carefully pushing these aside, she lifted her head pouring the gruel through cupped fists.

CHORUS *(chants until Darlene is seated)*: Spy. Spy. Spy. Spy. Spy. *(Man 1 grabs her, lifts her to her feet, plops her in chair center stage back. Man 2 still has back to audience.)*

CHORUS: American spy! American spy! War crimes against the Imperial Army! Spy! Spy! *(To each of these accusations, Darlene replies, "No!" with Men pulling her first one way, then the other.)*

DARLENE *(Falls to knees. Man 1 turns back.)*: I never shed a tear before those men, but when the guard had taken me back to my cell, I wept buckets. I would cry out to my God, "Oh, Lord, I can't go through another interrogation. I just can't."

CHORUS *(loud whisper)*: My grace is sufficient for thee.

DARLENE: "All right, O Lord. Just make me a good soldier for Jesus Christ." And He did. I went through another hearing, and another, finally—

MAN 1 *(turns and faces audience)*: You are accused, American spy. Your sentence: death by beheading! *(turns back)*

CHORUS: Death. Yes, yes, death. Death to spies. You shall die! Death to spies. Death. Death. YOU SHALL DIE!

(raise fists)

DARLENE: My inquisitors finally left me alone. I was so sick—dysentery, beriberi, cerebral malaria. One day during an attack of malaria, I thought, "If I could ony get a breath of air!"

(pantomimes rest of action, standing on chair)

WOMAN 1: With one foot on the doorknob, a push— she caught hold of the bars of the unboarded transom above the door.

WOMAN 2: She watched prisoners, jailed for minor misdemeanors, airing in the courtyard. Suddenly, a hand shot through the fence covered with Honolulu creeping vine. It held a big bunch of bananas.

WOMAN 1: A native woman who was standing nearby whisked them beneath her sarong, and no one knew she had them.

DARLENE *(drops from chair to floor, sits panting for breath)*: For months I have eaten nothing but watery gruel. Now I craved bananas. I could see them; I could taste them, smell them. "Oh, Lord," I prayed. "I'm not asking You for a whole bunch of bananas like that woman has. I'm just asking for one banana." Yet, think as I might, I could see it was impossible for the Lord to get a banana through those prison walls to me.

CHORUS: *(Feet marching softly. Man 1 turns around.)*

WOMAN 1: Many officers marched across the courtyard.

(Darlene rises, pulling herself up using the chair and steadies herself against it.)

WOMAN 2: Darlene prayed for strength to make the proper bow so she wouldn't receive a beating. The door opened. *(Man 2 faces audience.)*

DARLENE: Oh, my dear, Mr. Yamagi! *(claps her hands in delight)* It's just like seeing an old friend.

(Man 2 motions to Man 1. They move to stage right. Man 2 pantomimes discussion while Man 1 slowly lowers his head. They return shortly to Darlene.)

MAN 2: You're very ill, aren't you?

DARLENE: Yes, I am.

MAN 2: I'm going back to the camp now. Have you any word for the women?

DARLENE: Yes, sir. Tell them I'm all right. I'm still trusting the Lord. They'll know what I mean. *(Man 2 turns back, then Man 1. Darlene drops to the floor obviously exhausted.)*

CHORUS *(marching feet, softly)*

DARLENE: Suddenly I remembered I hadn't bowed to those men. I could hear they were coming again. "Oh, Lord," I prayed. "Why didn't You help me to remember? They're coming to beat me, and I can't stand another beating."

(Man 1 faces audience, turns away when Darlene speaks again.)

WOMAN 1: Then the door opened. The guard entered and spread on the floor—
WOMAN 2: Golden, yellow, beautiful . . .
DARLENE: Bananas! There were ninety-two bananas. In all my spiritual experience, I had never felt so ashamed before my Lord. I pushed them all into a corner and cried, "Oh, Lord. I couldn't even trust You for one banana. Look at them, almost one hundred."
CHORUS: That's how the Lord delights to give—with exceeding great abundance. That's how the Lord delights to give—above anything you ask or think.
DARLENE: The day I ate the last banana, the guards came again. *(Both men face audience.)*
MAN 2: We're taking you somewhere else.
DARLENE: We got into the limousine. If we turned left, I knew they were returning me to the concentration camp. But we turned right.
WOMAN 1: The car threaded through the streets of Macassar, and finally halted before the headquarters of the Secret Service Police.
WOMAN 2: Darlene Deibler was taken inside and given a large plate of beautiful white rice, kernels such as she had never seen. She knew it was her last meal.

(Man 1 steps forward.)

DARLENE *(steps forward beside Man 1)*: I was taken into the courtyard and stood before my executioner. He held a sheath of papers before me. They were the catalog of my supposed crimes.
MAN 1: You have been proven to be an American spy. Your sentence is death by beheading!
CHORUS: Death! Death! You shall die! Death to spies! Death to spies! You shall die! Death!

(Chorus raises fists on last shout. Man 1 pantomimes drawing long sword from sheath

at his side. Everyone freezes for long pause.)
WOMAN 1 *(whispering)*: I'll live for Him who died for me.
WOMAN 2 *(whispers slightly louder)*: I'll live for Him who died for me.
WOMEN 1 AND 2: I'll live for Him who died for me.
DARLENE: As my executioner raised his sword, the Spirit filled my heart with these words. "Lord," I whispered, "what a strange thought when I'm about to die." Suddenly, I heard a car screech to a halt. There was shouting, feet running across the tile floor. Someone grabbed me, pulled me outside to the waiting limousine.

I don't know what happened. I only know that God spared my life.
WOMAN 1: Darlene Deibler was returned to the labor camp.
WOMAN 2: Here she remained until the end of the war. She weighed 80 pounds. Her hair had turned white.
WOMAN 1: In the last year of imprisonment, the Allied planes dropped 5,000 incendiary bombs over the camp. These flames consumed her last remaining possessions.
DARLENE: Finally, it was over. We were notified that peace had been signed in Tokyo Bay aboard the U.S. battleship, *Missouri*, on September 2, 1945. I learned that Dr. Jaffray had also died—two months before the war's end, on a forced march.
(Darlene walks slowly to center stage front. Men and Women blend into Chorus.)
Arrangements were made to evacuate me along with military personnel aboard *The Catalina*, a flying boat.

The morning I stepped into a rowboat that was to transport me out to the anchored flying boat, a great bitterness began to poison me. Eight years before and a war away, I had come to these islands on my first wedding anniversary. Now rowing away from shore, I could think of nothing but two wooden crosses lost on some jungle hillside. Grimly, I whispered, "Lord, I don't care if I ever see this place again."

CHORUS *(waving, calling out as individuals and as if at a great distance)*: Good-bye. Farewell.

DARLENE *(turns slightly toward Chorus)*: Then turning, I saw on the shore, the believers—those who had come to know the Lord.

CHORUS *(sings)*: God be with you till we meet again. *(Hums rest, through verse and chorus. Have Darlene's voice overlap.)*

DARLENE: Christ touched that poison in me and changed it to sweetness. I called back *(calling and waving)*, "Yes, someday I will come home again. I will come home." As the *Catalina* lifted airward carrying me from the jungle and swamps, the coastlines and mountains, I thought, "Lord, I didn't come to the Dutch East Indies because I was the wife of Russell Deibler. I didn't even come because of the needs of these people. I came because it was You who called me here. I will continue to follow You always."

PAUL

Dramatic Biblical play for teens
by Jeanne Murray Walker

This Biblically based drama, written for junior high and high school, portrays the life-changing power of God as demonstrated in the apostle Paul's life.

Cast of Characters:
Narrator
Antiochus
Publicus
Gamaliel
Saul
Mary
Stephanie
Peter
Ananias
Servant
Barnabas
Man
Woman
Crowd
Messenger

ACT I SCENE I

NARRATOR: It is Thursday evening in Jerusalem. Coolness has come with dusk. Sweaty and tired people have walked to the Temple after the stinging hot day. In the Temple, friends meet and small boys rush noisily to their classes. Money changers at the door add to the confusion with their cries. Crafty old men sell pigeons and doves for sacrifices. The tinkle of money rises over the buzz of the people. In a room of the Temple a meeting of the Sanhedrin is in session. The men are the guiding body of the Jewish religion. They sit around a table talking.

(Have four men dressed in upper-class robes of Jesus' day sitting at a table talking.)

ANTIOCHUS: A carpenter from Nazareth! A carpenter, you say? And all this trouble?

PUBLICUS: Haven't men like lowly carpenters and brickmakers been claiming they were the Messiah for hundreds of years?

GAMALIEL: Oh, yes. The people believe them for a while, but it doesn't last long. *(slowly, with thought)* I'm an old man now, and I can remember many times when common men have claimed to be the Messiah. Ha! Some people always believe them. Then they die. And their followers go back to their work as if it had never happened.

ANTIOCHUS *(angrily)*: Ignorant people!

GAMALIEL *(looking at him sternly)*: They're your people. Pity them. They want some word from God. They get stirred up easily and— and then they forget easily. They have hot blood.

PUBLICUS: But what do you say about this new movement, Gamaliel?

GAMALIEL: Leave the people alone. They'll forget that Nazarene carpenter soon enough. He's dead.

SAUL *(hotly)*: We're fools! Listen. He's been dead for several years. He has more followers now than He had when He was alive. This cult is spreading like spilled water.

GAMALIEL *(laughing kindly)*: What did I say? Look at Saul. He certainly has hot blood!

SAUL *(ignoring him)*: I'm telling you, if we don't do something, the Sanhedrin will no longer be the guide for the people. Everyone

will believe those fishermen who come to our synagogues and talk about Him.
PUBLICUS: Well, Gamaliel, I have learned everything I know from you. Yes, indeed. You—
ANTIOCHUS (*cutting in on Publicus*): We all have. We all have. What does that have to do with it?
PUBLICUS: Well, you understand, I don't want to go against your judgment, but—
ANTIOCHUS: —you think we should do something? You agree with Saul?
PUBLICUS: Begging your pardon, Gamaliel, but I do.
ANTIOCHUS (*to Publicus*): Well, what? What can we do without the Roman government standing behind us?
SAUL (*in a low voice*): Listen, whether we have the Roman government behind us or not, we have to do something. Do you know who Stephen is? One of their leaders. He's out there right now, telling the people about that reformer, Jesus. Can you imagine? He says the Man came alive again after He died.
PUBLICUS: If you don't mind my saying so, we don't need to let that go on. We're in charge of the Temple, you know.
ANTIOCHUS: Is he the man you were arguing with the other day, Saul?
SAUL (*embarrassed*): Yes . . .
ANTIOCHUS: How did you do? He's not educated. He must have made a fool of himself.
SAUL: Well . . .
PUBLICUS: It really seemed to me that he was quite smart. Yes, indeed. Quite quick and . . .
ANTIOCHUS: He beat you, Saul? No!
GAMALIEL: Perhaps that's why our young friend wants to get rid of him. He's not used to losing an argument. Eh, Saul?
SAUL (*angry*): No. If he was right, if he was arguing for the truth, then I would be glad if he could beat me. But he's not, and right now he's convincing people that God is not God—that Jesus is God. That's why we have

to do something. In the name of Heaven we can't let this go on.

GAMALIEL: Ah, young friend, perhaps you are right after all. Perhaps we should do something about this Stephen. Make him an example, maybe?

SCENE II

(Mary, a woman of about 45 with gray hair, is talking with Stephanie, a girl in her late teens, who is very pretty. They are in Mary's home, which is simple. There is little furniture except some crude chairs, and the door is on the left.)

MARY: But he is with God—
STEPHANIE: Of course he is with God. And Jesus.
MARY: Jesus. I'd like to see Jesus again.
STEPHANIE: I never saw Him. Peter has told me so much about how He used to heal sick people and pray sometimes all night. I know my uncle is with Jesus, but we needed him here. He was so strong—
MARY *(sighing)*: I know.
STEPHANIE *(gesticulating)*: And, Mary, they hated him so much. So unfairly. What did he ever do to them? And they stoned him.
MARY *(laughs a little)*: Sometimes I think they finally killed him because he could talk so well they were afraid he would convince them Jesus was God.
STEPHANIE *(laughs)*: Oh, he could have!

(A knock is heard. Mary goes to the door, looks out cautiously.)

MARY: Peter!
PETER: Well, may I come in?
MARY: Of course. *(Peter steps in.)*
PETER: Oh, Stephanie. How are you?
STEPHANIE: I'm lonesome for my uncle, Peter.
PETER *(sits down)*: God must have wanted him, Stephanie. Strange. Stephen was one of our most convincing men . . . *(thoughtfully)* God will have to look very far before He finds a man with more fire than your uncle.
MARY *(looking at Peter closely)*: Peter, you look tired.

Are you well? What is it?
PETER: They're always after us, Mary. Not the Roman government, but our own Jewish people. Now it's that little man who stirred up the trouble for Stephen.
MARY: Saul of Tarsus?
PETER: That's the man.
MARY: What now?
PETER: He's going to Damascus with a band of soldiers.
STEPHANIE (sighs, relieved): I'm glad he's leaving here.
PETER: No. He's going for the believers there. He's going to bring them back to stand trial here.
STEPHANIE: May God help them!
MARY (alarmed): But, Peter, there are so many believers in Damascus!
PETER (sadly gets up and walks around the room): Yes. He heard that dozens of them moved there after they stoned Stephen.
MARY: That man has done more to hurt us believers than the rest of the Jewish nation put together.
PETER: He's a man of unbelievable energy. If he could only love as strongly as he hates.
STEPHANIE (suddenly jumping up): But we have to warn them in Damascus. They can leave the city—
PETER: No, no. It's too late. He's on the road already. It's too late for anything except prayer.

SCENE III

(*Paul is sitting in the corner of a simple house. His eyes are closed, and he is motionless. The furniture in the room consists of two long couches. The door is on the right. Ananias, an old man who is stooped and gray, walks slowly into the room and approaches Paul.*)

ANANIAS: Saul! Brother!
PAUL (*looks up*): How did you know my name?
ANANIAS: I saw Jesus in a vision.
PAUL (*eagerly*): I, too!
ANANIAS: He told me to come here and welcome you as a brother in Him.
PAUL: You see I am blind, but that is not all. I am different somehow.

ANANIAS: I was afraid to come here. I had heard that you were coming to Damascus to put all of us believers in chains.

PAUL: I used to be burning with hate for people who believed Jesus was God. But I have met Jesus now—I have seen that He truly is God.

ANANIAS: You must tell me what changed you. But first God has told me to give you back your sight.

(He kneels by Paul and touches his eyes very simply.)

PAUL *(shakes his head)*: Ah! *(opens his eyes and looks around wonderingly)* Three days I have been walking around with someone leading me—like a blind man. And now I can see.

ANANIAS: That's a sign from God. He has power. Perhaps now you realize how much.

PAUL: It's so strange. I came to this city hating the Man I now call Lord. How can I understand it?

ANANIAS *(laughing)*: Jesus happened to you, brother! You must get your wits about you and tell me how it happened. But you must be hungry! Come. I'll have the servant get you something to eat. *(He motions to the servant standing just outside the door, and then they speak in low tones. The servant goes out. Ananias points to one of the couches, and they sit down.)* All right. I am ready to listen.

PAUL: It was strange. We were on the road between here and Jerusalem. We were getting close to Damascus. Suddenly I saw a brilliant light flash from somewhere in the sky. *(He turns to Ananias.)* It was like lightning aimed at my eyes. I think I fell down on the road. And a Voice said, "Why are you hurting Me?"

ANANIAS *(excited)*: Could you talk?

PAUL: I asked who the Voice was—

ANANIAS: And?

PAUL *(wonderingly)*: And the Voice told me that He was Jesus. Jesus! The One who was killed.

ANANIAS: The One who rose from His tomb.

PAUL: Yes . . . yes. And the Voice told me to come here so I could learn more. That was three days ago. All this time I have been blind, and I haven't eaten anything.

ANANIAS *(laughing)*: Then I'm glad I spoke to the servant about getting some food! I know the look of a hungry man when I see One.

(Paul laughs.)

ANANIAS: Brother, what are you going to do now?

PAUL *(slowly)*: Now? Now, I'm going to spend the rest of my life fighting just as hard for the cause of Jesus as I used to fight against it. That is all I know. I have had three days to think. I need more.

ANANIAS: More time? Why?

PAUL: I know nothing about the Man I call God. *(turns to Ananias abruptly)* I have to learn about the One whose voice I heard.

ANANIAS: But you have been in the best schools. Didn't you study under Gamaliel? Surely you've heard about the things Jesus did?

PAUL *(waving his hand)*: I learned about the God of our fathers. And I learned about the Greek gods—

ANANIAS: Nothing about Jesus?

PAUL: Gamaliel laughed at believers and said the cult would not last any longer than cults that grew up around some of the other reformers that called themselves the Messiah. No. I didn't learn anything of His works, really. If I am going to tell other people about Him, I have to learn about Him myself!

ANANIAS: Whatever God tells you, brother. *(bowing his head)* Perhaps you will someday be as strong for the cause as Stephen was. Maybe you are the man God has found to take his place.

ACT II SCENE I

(Mary is in her house at Jerusalem, sitting on a chair, sewing.

A knock is heard at the door. She goes to it and looks out cautiously.)

PETER: Mary! Let me in!
MARY *(opens the door)*: Peter! What is it?
PETER: More bad news. *(He comes into the room.)*
MARY *(smiling)*: I am almost used to it.
PETER: It's Paul.
MARY: Paul? What could be wrong? He's not here in Jerusalem. He should be in Iconium preaching right now.
PETER *(excitedly)*: Exactly. Exactly. And the Jews are talking about stoning him.
MARY *(puts her hands over her eyes, sinks down on a chair)*: Stone him? What for?
PETER *(sighs, sitting down)*: Oh, he's been preaching in the synagogue there. So many people have believed . . . but the ones that haven't—
MARY: —want to kill him.
PETER: Exactly! The whole town is divided. Some are for him. The believers, of course. And the Jewish leaders are against him.
MARY: But how do you know this, Peter? We're a long way from Iconium.
PETER: Paul sent a messenger back asking us to pray.
MARY *(sitting down thoughtfully)*: They want to stone him . . . like Stephen.
PETER: Yes. Like Stephen. *(He gets up quickly.)* But we must find the others. Come on. Paul sent his message so we would pray. *(They both hurry out.)*

SCENE II

(It is afternoon in Lystra. In the foreground sits a man who is crippled. In the background stand people of the town, talking. Barnabas and Paul stroll down the street.)

BARNABAS: I suppose we had to leave Iconium, but work there was just starting.
PAUL: Yes, Barnabas, the believers at Jerusalem must have prayed for us. I feel so certain it was God's will for us to leave.
BARNABAS: And come to this town. Look at that man.

PAUL *(stops, looks)*: He's listening to us. If he wants to hear what we're saying, why doesn't he come closer?

BARNABAS *(also stopping)*: He's strange looking . . . they're ignoring him, the people. Look! I don't believe he can move. He's crippled. Look at his feet.

PAUL *(suddenly)*: Come on. *(They walk toward the man.)* Get up on your feet. You can walk. *(The man looks confused, and then jumps to his feet. As he does so, all the people stop talking and look at him, then at Paul and Barnabas. They are silent with surprise. Suddenly one man steps out and says in a loud, excited voice:)*

LYSTRIAN MAN: I know! These two are gods! How else could they do this?

(The people gasp as though a bomb were thrown onto the street. A few of them advance and touch Paul and Barnabas.)

LYSTRIAN MAN: They are! They are! They've come down from Mount Olympus! The one is Zeus and the other is Hermes.

A WOMAN: Let's offer sacrifices.

CROWD: Yes, let's offer sacrifices!

PAUL *(to Barnabas)*: I don't understand. *(loudly)* Listen, we're not gods. We're men the same as you are.

CROWD *(louder)*: Zeus and Hermes! Let's offer them sacrifices!

PAUL: Listen! We came here to tell you about the real God. *(The crowd murmurs.)* We tell you, we're not gods. We have come to tell you about Jesus, God's Son. Jehovah is the only God. He has proved His power to you and your grandfathers by sending you rain and sun day after day. Jehovah is the only God, and Jesus is His Son.

SCENE III

(Mary, Stephanie, and Peter sit talking together at Mary's house. A knock is heard. Stephanie goes to the door, and lets the man in. He is a messenger.)

PETER: I have seen you before, brother.

MESSENGER: Yes. I come from the church at Antioch.

MARY (*smiling*): How are the believers there?

MESSENGER: Paul is with us.

PETER: Paul?

MESSENGER: I bring news from him.

PETER (*gets up excitedly*): Tell us quickly. How is he?

MESSENGER (*solemnly*): He was badly hurt, but is now recovering.

MARY: Badly hurt!

STEPHANIE: Recovering?

PETER: How?

MARY: Where?

MESSENGER: When he was in Lystra he walked the streets and preached. And he healed a man who couldn't walk. He and Barnabas—

PETER (*laughing*): Paul can't keep quiet. He preaches his way down the streets. He can't even wait for a synagogue!

MARY (*smiling*): Hush, Peter! (*to the messenger*) Go on.

MESSENGER: A crowd of people were standing around, and they saw Paul heal the man. They were sure Paul and Barnabas were Zeus and—

STEPHANIE (*laughing gleefully*): No! But they're old gods who are only in legends. Everybody knows they aren't alive.

MESSENGER: The people in Lystra thought Zeus and Hermes had walked right down from Mount Olympus into the streets.

PETER: Imagine what Paul thought!

MESSENGER: Of course Paul and Barnabas said they weren't. They told them that Jesus was God's Son. The people almost started a sacrifice right there in the street. But people are changeable. A few days later some Jews came from Antioch and Iconium and accused Paul. The people picked up stones and stoned Paul.

MARY: And Barnabas.

MESSENGER: No, no, not Barnabas.

STEPHANIE: They stoned Paul. And he watched while they stoned my uncle!

MESSENGER: And then the

95

people left him, thinking he was dead.

PETER: Dead?

MESSENGER: He was badly hurt, but not dead. He is in Antioch now, and he soon hopes to come here.

MARY: We will see him again!

MESSENGER: You will see him again. And he tells you to keep fighting the good fight.

PETER: Paul! He would say that after he was nearly stoned to death!

MARY: Do you have any more news?

MESSENGER: No more. And I must hurry on, because I have business in Jerusalem. *(He goes to the door. Mary goes with him.)*

MARY: You will be going back?

MESSENGER: Tomorrow.

MARY: Send him news that we are fighting the good fight.

MESSENGER: I will tell him.

(He goes out the door. Mary walks back thoughtfully. Peter gets up and paces around the room.)

PETER: You know, sometimes I think that man has fire in his veins instead of blood.

MARY: Jesus is with him.

STEPHANIE: Perhaps my uncle did not die for nothing. Paul was watching. And Paul has taken his place.